To Jay

May you always
have Love &
Happiness
in your
heart.
Jonathan

David

Also by David Lamb

Platanos Y Collard Greens

www.platanosandcollardgreens.com

Praise for *Platanos Y Collard Greens*

"A modern day West Side Story... has developed a huge following among people who come to see it again and again."
THE NEW YORK TIMES

"A play that everyone can relate to... a Hip-Hop drama... incorporating humor and utilizing extraordinary, moving, and explosive poetry. [This play] wins on all levels: it entertains, educates, and leaves one satisfied."
THE NEW YORK AMSTERDAM NEWS

"Tells the story of a Black man and Latina woman forced to defend their love against cultural and racial prejudices."
THE DAILY NEWS

"*Platanos Y Collard Greens* is sweet, true fun! Bring your appetite for laughter when you go to see this novella set on stage!"
LA DIVA LATINA® MAGAZINE

Perfect Combination

Seven Key Ingredients to Happily Living and Loving Together

Between The Lines Productions
New York

PERFECT COMBINATION

The authors are grateful for permission to use an excerpt from the following previously copyrighted material:

David Lamb, King of the World.

Layout and cover design by Zachary Fabri.
Library of Congress Cataloging-in-Publication Data has been applied for.
ISBN: 978-0-9849250-0-1

Jamillah and David Lamb

WITH KEVIN TAYLOR

I dedicate this book to my extraordinary loving grandmother and best friend, Hunabuna, who one year promised me that I would meet the love of my life by Spring. And I did!

Jamillah Lamb

I dedicate this book to my mother, Saundra Lamb, the most shining example of unconditional love I have ever known.

David Lamb

TABLE OF CONTENTS

INTRODUCTION

We're In This Love Together

❦

Whe spend almost every waking hour with each other.

Working in theater and running our business together demands all of our time—whether it's being at a radio station for a 6 a.m. interview, being at the theater at 10 p.m. for rehearsal, or hosting weekend salsa lessons with audience members (trying to put some soul in our four left feet). Our lives are lived together.

For the past eight years, we've been blessed to have thousands of couples enjoy and be moved by *Platanos Y Collard Greens*, our hilarious tale of two college students who fall in love, until her mother finds out and has a heart attack! We've had the enormous pleasure of watching the audience laugh till it hurts, of hearing them tell us how much the story reminds them of their families and their experiences, and how it leaves them feeling triumphant, knowing love conquers all.

Over the years, when we've gone on stage at the end of the show and introduced ourselves as the producers, the audience is usually shocked! They simply can't believe that we (a married couple) are not only the ones behind the play—but that we work together on a daily basis—and have not only not killed each other under the strain of running a business together, but that our love has grown stronger. And nine times out of ten, they are not only shocked—but demand to know our secret!

As a result, we have informally become relationship counselors for more people than we could have ever imagined. For years, radio hosts have encouraged us to write our story and share the keys we have found to having it all—Love and Happiness, living together, working together and most of all happily, joyfully loving together.

Traveling this road has taught us, and continues to teach us, that to thrive as a couple (not just survive), we have to be on the same page—or have peace about the places in our lives where we are not (and trust us, there are some).

When you think about it, every couple works together! Just because you don't share an office, don't think for a minute that this book doesn't apply to you. Have you ever planned a party together? How about a trip? Have you ever negotiated who's going to drop off the kids at school? Or at whose house you're spending Thanksgiving—your mother's or his? If you have, you work together.

Being together all day, in all things, has helped us stay focused on the goals that we have in our individual lives and the goals that we have for our relationship and our family. We are by no means claiming to be the champions of love, but we will say without shame that we are cheerleaders for love. And the guidelines we present in this book are the tools that have helped us. We offer these ingredients, these lessons that we have learned (and continue to learn), to help couples begin the conversation—expand it or fine-tune it—in the life-long, love-long quest to make relationships work on the road to Love and Happiness.

Part guidebook and part journal, Perfect Combination opens the conversation to discovering the key ingredients that will help you learn from the lessons of your life to create your own recipe for Love and Happiness.

Sincerely and with Love,
Jamillah & David Lamb

CHAPTER ONE

Ready For Love

We've all heard it before, in a hundred different ways:
Don't worry about the past. Live for today.
No doubt this is great advice, but we've always wanted
to ask, as perhaps you have, how do you do it?

So many couples don't want to deal with it, especially not in detail, but we all come to every relationship with a past. We walk around carrying hurts, pains and regrets in gigantic emotional duffel bags. Believe us; we do the same, just like every other couple. Just because you see us on stage smiling at each other affectionately at the end of a great show, our genuine love on display, doesn't mean that we haven't had to unload emotional baggage to arrive at a place of Love and Happiness. So before we get into what works in our relationship and in our partnership, or deal with the places where we are still being challenged, we wanted to share with you our "Before You" talk.

We have all been in relationships before that didn't work, and we all have to deal with the ideas, memories, expectations and pain that keep us from Love and Happiness. It's necessary because there are some important lessons you learned in those other relationships about what you don't want and will not accept in a relationship (your deal-breakers). But, here's the truth that stings: even though you're an amazing, wonderful, gifted person, you have also learned some things about yourself that didn't always reflect you in the best light, but they were real.

In order to be willing to move forward, in love, with love, you've got to deal with what you've learned about yourself. The lessons you learned are important and it's essential to incorporate them into your everyday thinking so that you don't make those same mistakes or waste time on those same conversations, when you know that you already know better.

This chapter is about the things, including the emotional baggage (the hurts, pains, insecurities and beliefs that were holding us back), that we learned about ourselves before we met, warts and all. It is the starting point. So you can see, if we can do it, you're already halfway home.

I Wanted To Prove I Was My Own Woman... So I Put Every Guy Through The Ringer!

» *Jamillah*

When I was growing up, I'm not sure that I really knew myself. I knew that there were certain things about myself that I did understand. I was a smart girl. But like a lot of young girls, I didn't really know *myself*. I knew I was creative, but it was buried inside of me. So much was buried inside of me because I was raised to be a good girl. As a good girl, I wasn't raised to be perfect, as much as I was raised to do the right thing. I was told that I needed to have a "proper career" and I knew that there were certain things that were expected of me. I was expected to be responsible and to have good grades and to be a respectable daughter.

I was raised on the South Side of Chicago in a working class neighborhood. I went to the same elementary school and high school as First Lady Michelle Obama (though not at the same time). My mother and stepfather raised me and my three brothers and my sister, and they gave us great morals and great education. But as I grew older, I felt I needed something more. I needed confidence. Raised with strict parents who were also poor, I had to wear modest clothing (think ankle length skirts) that was sometimes bought from the Salvation Army. In high school, I most often felt like the odd girl out. Combined with my shy nature, even though I had a few girlfriends, I usually felt alone and insecure about my looks, my personality and generally about myself.

When I graduated high school, I looked forward to college as a chance to spread my wings and blossom. Because my parents had always stressed academics, they introduced me to top tier colleges—even arranging family trips to allow me to visit campuses. At first, I wanted to attend Columbia University because I had had a love affair with New York City, ever since visiting my grandmother in New Jersey in the summers. But after staying for a long weekend on Columbia's campus, I knew I wasn't quite ready for the Big Apple on my own. Instead I chose Wesleyan University in a small town in Connecticut, which was close to my family in New Jersey and still close enough to NYC.

During my junior year, I received a letter from my biological father, my first-ever communication with him. I was very hesitant for a few reasons; I wasn't sure what to expect since I had never spoken to or even seen a picture of this man. I wasn't sure what feelings it would bring up and if I would be able to handle the possible anger and resentment I might feel. I also wasn't sure how it would make my mother and stepfather who raised me feel. But over time, I dealt with these feelings and my relationship with my father eventually developed; from letters to phone calls to an in-person meeting, and our friendship grew. In fact, after college and graduate school, I moved from the east coast to California to get to know him better. Developing that relationship helped me to stop being so analytical and in my head about life. He is what I would call a free spirit.

> I was so hell bent on not being controlled that *if a man tried to do anything for me*, from buying dinner to buying a token for the subway, *I would lose it*. I'm not kidding. As one unfortunate victim who skipped watching the Super Bowl, to go on our first date, experienced when he made the mistake of buying my subway token and dropping it in the slot at the turnstile. *Jamillah*

Before moving in with my father, I was trying to rebel against the way of thinking that made me believe that men thought I was a woman who needed to be rescued or controlled by their actions. I'd had enough of being someone's daughter and being told what role I was supposed to play in life. My rebellion definitely showed up in my dating life, causing me to scrutinize every action and every gesture to be sure that the guy trying to win my heart was not also trying to direct my steps. I felt that I had a lot to discover about myself. I needed to do it on my own and not under the watchful eye of a man.

When I moved to California, I was able to explore my love of the arts, especially painting. I was able to allow myself to be freer in expressing myself. I was able to see that there was a part of me that was creative and not just cerebral. I discovered that I was funny (not stand-up comedy level, but I'm pretty funny when I get going) and that I had lots of things that I was good at—but I also found out that there were areas where I needed to lighten up.

Despite this growing realization that I did need to lighten up, I couldn't stop myself from putting every guy who tried to get to know me through the ringer. I wanted him to see that he couldn't order my every step, nor direct my every whim and that I didn't need him to lead me, take care of me or fulfill some fairytale fantasy that I believed he believed every little girl had about every little boy. I wanted to prove that I was my own woman. There is a guy or two who might still be recovering from the verbal lashing that he took from me while I was "gaining my independence". I was really just trying to assert myself (and my growth) to my parents, but that assertiveness spilled over into my first few clumsy attempts at a relationship. I'm sure that when we first met, it might have even tried to spill over into my relationship with David, especially in those early days of dating. With his flippant New York demeanor, though, he probably didn't even notice. I'm thankful about that.

I don't think he realized it at the time, but when we met, I was at war with myself. I had been living in California for a year and I was still not able to stop myself from feeling insecure about my ability to be in a relationship without feeling controlled. I wanted to be in a relationship and feel beautiful and loved, but I also wanted to be independent and self-assured. Slowly, I'd begun to realize that every guy wasn't trying to control the situation. Some men are simply raised to be gentlemen and believe that they should do certain things for women. They can do those things and still respect a woman for being independent and smart and having her own perspective.

Let Him Care About You - *What I needed to know about myself was that I could be with someone who cared about me and who wanted to care for me— and it didn't mean that I was weak.*

Being able to allow someone to do something for you is not a commentary on your strengths or weaknesses. It's a commentary on someone's care and concern for you. I'm not suggesting that there aren't people out there who are controlling because we all know that there are. I am also not saying that there aren't people out there who want someone to come along and take care of everything because they are out there, too.

"A WIF"

Even after we were married, for the first few years, I did not want to be called a wife. **I teasingly told David I was a "Wif" (Wife with no e)***. To me a wife was someone whose whole life revolved around cooking and cleaning for her man. I now understand what my aunt meant when she told me a few weeks after my wedding "Be a good wife." She meant be that person who makes him happy and who he can rely on, and doing that doesn't mean giving up any part of myself.* **Jamillah**

That's simply not me; yet I had to realize that allowing my husband to be his own man wasn't some generalized submission to me letting him be The Man. I had to learn to let him be his own man, my man, the only man in the relationship. That doesn't mean that he's stronger or better in the relationship. It doesn't mean anything other than we both have our skills and talents where we excel. We also both have our own perspective on life and I had to let go of my old views on others in order to genuinely see things from his perspective.

SHE SAYS:
"LET GO!"

> *You can never see the potential of your future, if you are always viewing it through the lens of your past.*

As a woman, I had to learn that you can never see the potential of your future, if you are always viewing it through the lens of your past. I learned that I had to accept my husband and the qualities he was bringing to our relationship. I had to see and appreciate what he was actually offering me and my life and not be overly-concerned with what I imagined his intentions were. I had to be in this relationship and watch it flourish. For me, that meant not getting ahead of it or ahead of myself. I had to learn to slow down and absorb and really listen to what he was saying in the moment and not be defensive or read into it or hear some other voice from my past, rather than hearing him.

Every morning I tell myself: don't put him through the ringer. Let him care about you. Let go.

Wow.

When I thought about this first chapter, I didn't think I would have to dig as deep as I was asked. I thought I had great lessons to pass on and that, with my wife, we could write a book that would be helpful to men and women, giving people some perspective from both sides of the conversation—and it would be pretty easy. Then we started talking and I had to ask and answer some pretty tough questions.

I thought I was a pretty cool dude growing up. I was raised in New York City and I had my street sense about me, meaning that I could get around town and be around anybody, anywhere and feel like I could handle myself. Big cities can give you that kind of braggadocio and New Yorkers are known for it. So I thought I was a guy who had his stuff together and could handle whatever life threw at me. And then I went to Princeton.

I was a fish out of water. Being at a wealthy Ivy League school brought up some real issues for me, especially class insecurities and immaturity, and it showed in the ways I interacted with people, especially women.

I grew up poor, in the public housing projects of Astoria, Queens. I went to public school, and when I graduated high school, I headed straight into the City's University system. Hunter College is an excellent, but working class school. In short, all of my life had been spent in environments where working class people were in the majority. But at Princeton, I was a poor kid on a campus with the wealthiest kids on the east coast. Insecurity about being a poor kid combined with my suspicious nature converged to make a young man who wasn't very comfortable in his skin.

I Was More Suspicious Than Columbo!

I grew up with people who could be suspicious of others. That's probably a trait that many New Yorkers possess. I wondered why people thought certain things about me or thought they could treat me a certain way. I come from a family of people who taught me suspicion as a survival mechanism. Unfortunately, at times, I employed that tactic in relationships. I wondered about the intentions of any woman I was dating. Why was she with me? If I couldn't line it up with my shaky self-confidence, I exited stage right as quickly as possible. I am not proud to say it, but I have ended relationships for reasons so ridiculous that if I hadn't been the one who'd done it, I wouldn't believe anyone could be that foolish—but I was!

I hope that these women aren't spending any energy trying to figure out what they did wrong. I am taking ownership for it right now—IT IS ME! I was a man who was struggling with his place in life, especially after I had thought it was pretty clear.

> **Suspicions**
> Suspicion can be encoded into the DNA of relationships—sometimes to ridiculous extremes. Think of all of the economically malnourished guys you know who take Kanye's Golddigger as their gospel, even though they haven't so much as been able to pay for dinner and a movie in ten years.

Many black men grow up having heard that women can't be trusted. But the truth is, that's not the real suspicion that plagues so many. The real root of this suspicious feeling is connected to growing up in poor communities, believing that people are trying to get over on you and want to keep you down! Unfortunately the belief that the system is trying to get you infects and corrupts our relationships; I have seen it in

Real love always catches you off-guard.

myself and dozens of men. We substitute suspicion of the system with suspicion of the one we ultimately need to trust most.

Suspicion can be encoded into the DNA of relationships—sometimes to ridiculous extremes. This perpetual suspicion causes us to constantly wonder and second guess why a woman is with us. That's the first question we often hear from fathers about their daughters' suitors. So naturally when you let suspicion and self-doubt get the best of you, you start to ask it about yourself—"Why does she want to be with me!"

While I was at Princeton, I dated a woman from a middle-class family who I thought had reason to think she was better than me. I still dated her, but the question kept popping up in my mind: "Why do you want to be with me?" So in order not to have to deal with or suffer the embarrassment of her eventually dumping me—because I could never live up to what I imagined

I was going to have to grow up and grow into feeling what love felt like or I was going to end up by myself.

to be her middle-class, bourgeois fantasies of what a boyfriend and future husband should be, I broke up with her. I remember her especially because I saw her reading SELF ® magazine one day. When we broke up, I wrote a letter (yup, not even face-to-face or over the phone) and told this beautiful, young African-American woman, "You will never know yourself reading SELF ® magazine!" (To top it off, I had the nerve to wonder why she didn't want to speak to me after I'd had second thoughts about breaking up with her!) I was always looking for ways and theories for why people did what they did because I didn't ever want to be caught off-guard. That's kind of funny when you think about it because real love always catches you off-guard.

I was running from love because I was trying to run from the feelings of being vulnerable, which played out in feeling insecure, wondering why any woman would really want to be with me, a kid from the projects. I hadn't even thought about or made room for the idea of love. I didn't hear a lot about love growing up. I saw it in my family and in movies, but I didn't know what it was supposed to feel like on the inside. I thought it was supposed to be easy and feel better and when it felt uncomfortable, I bolted. I realized that I was going to have to grow up and grow into feeling what love felt like or I was going to end up by myself. I had to learn to reign in and to let go of my suspicious nature, especially when I found myself in love with the woman I knew I was going to marry. It wasn't easy. I worked on it and sometimes, I still have to work on it. But she has such a kind heart and a sweet spirit that I knew that the self-doubt and suspicion would kill us.

This was a relationship I didn't want to see die.

HE SAYS
"TRUST YOUR CHOICES"

Somebody once said that *"all is fair in love and war"* but I want you to know that LOVE ISN'T WAR! We have to let go of the rules of engagement and the tactics that are war-like because if you don't, you'll never know what it feels like to have peace—neither peace of mind, and definitely not peace in a loving relationship with an amazing person.

Let go of the idea to treat love like war, because that's a battle that has no victors.

My wife is my best friend and I trust her with my life. I am thankful every day, because my relationship with her has helped me learn to trust my own choices. If I was suspicious of anything in our relationship, I had to deal with the fact that what I was really doing was being doubtful and unsure of my own choice. I had to let go of a lot of my insecurities from my days as a young man and I had to let go of some of what I learned from men in my own family and in my community. Most of all I had to let go of the idea to treat love like war, because that's a battle that has no victors.

Jamillah growing up in Chicago.

A chubby little Lamb.

David meets his namesake.

Jamillah when she was auditioning for the Jackson 5.

David back when his grandmother called him her little goat because he never combed his hair.

Jamillah always loved junk food.

OUR KEY INGREDIENT:

✿

Let Your Past Be Your Past

2 Cups of Being in the Moment

1 Cup of Forgiveness

1 Tablespoon of Humor

Each day with love is new. So any chance that you get to love, take full advantage of it.

All of us have made some bad choices and thought they were good choices at the time. We have all been hurt and some of us have hurt others, but that is the past. When you get a new chance at love, you have to treat it like it's new.

Along the way, if you get to meet some of the people you knew when you were working through your struggles with love and learning yourself, apologize to them so that they know it wasn't them; it was just you working out your own stuff.

We now know that before we met each other and fell in love neither of us really knew what it felt like to be in love. If some of you are reading this book with your first love or your greatest love, it may help you to remember the key ingredient to being in a relationship is to be in *this* relationship.

Whatever you did, whatever you endured, whatever you suffered or caused somebody else to suffer before you got into the space where you could say that you are clearly ready for love, be willing to forgive that. Dr. Maya Angelou says, "When you know better, you do better." Now, move forward and do love… better.

END OF CHAPTER PLAYLIST

Chapter One — Ready for Love

1. **Ready For Love** by India Arie

2. **Wanna Be Loved** by Buju Banton

3. **Joy and Pain** by Maze, featuring Frankie Beverly

4. **Wait For Love** by Luther Vandross

5. **Is This Love** by Bob Marley

CHAPTER TWO

Vision of Love

There is sweetness, a great sense of assurance, in your soul, when you KNOW that you've connected with the right person.

Yes, there may be some issues that you have to work through, within yourself and between each other, to be able to be sure that you're sure, but when you know, you just know.

We both remember *knowing* right away. But the *way* we remember knowing is different. That's a beautiful thing. It reminds us that, like most men and women, what we hold as special in our hearts are different parts of those early days.

Memories Matter

We've learned that we may not always remember something the other person can't forget, or we may not always remember the same thing the same way and we're cool with that—now. But there was a time when we would spend far too much time and way too much energy trying to prove which of us was right! Until time, experience, love and exhaustion taught us—WE'RE BOTH RIGHT.

So many times the woman will remember the date of the first kiss, but the man will remember the corner it was on. They each remembered a detail that made it special for them. If you get lost in your own need to be right or so caught up in your own need to make a fact important, you could dismiss what your partner holds dear about your relationship.

So, this part of our story isn't about our first date or when we first saw each other. It's really about how each of us thinks differently. We can still have what's important to us, and even if that may not hold the same importance to our partner, that doesn't make it unimportant.

Remember, you love each other and love *is* in the details. You just remember different details. And that's a beautiful thing.

» *Jamillah*

What I remember most about meeting David is everything. At the time, I was working at the Low Income Investment Fund, where I had been working for about a year. David came to San Francisco for a company retreat with the rest of the New York City staff. I have to admit that there was an instant attraction. It was electric. I couldn't take my eyes off him.

> *David*

Naturally.

> *Jamillah*

Anyway, we were in a conference room, gathered around to see what the 2-day event was going to entail, when we locked eyes for a bit. Sometime during that day, one of his co-workers, Valerie, had decided that David and I would be a good fit. She was pushing him in my direction to get to know me, and she was hard at work trying to find out details about me on her own. She was so persistent it was like she was a one-woman matchmaking service!

> *David*

She was my agent.

> *Jamillah*

Later that evening, a bunch of us from the office were going to a restaurant (a really entertaining and colorful Thai restaurant). We were sitting at a long table and I could see him jockeying to try to get the spot directly across from me. He was negotiating with his co-workers and I pretended not to notice. I noticed. How could I not? He nearly near knocked poor Valerie out of her seat and onto the floor so he could sit across from me.

» David

She knew she wasn't supposed to be taking that seat.

» Jamillah

After dinner, people from my office decided to go out dancing, so I asked David if he wanted to go. He said no. He said that he was jet-lagged, but I thought it meant that he wasn't really interested. If he was interested, he wouldn't have offered such a corny answer. That's what I felt because he hadn't jumped at the chance. Despite my hunch that he wasn't really interested, I didn't completely write him off. Before the weekend was over, we got to speak and I told him that I had family in New Jersey and that I went to the east coast sometimes to visit them.

Love Jones

It was like a scene from *Love Jones*. I mean who doesn't love *Love Jones*, and the closing scene after she reads her poem at the café and they kiss in the street under the rain. Magic.

Jamillah's Favorite Movies

Love Jones
The Five Heartbeats
Grease
Stand By Me
The Wood

David's Favorite Movies

Spartacus
Cooley High
Planet of the Apes
Shawshank Redemption
Glory

When I came to visit my family around the 4th of July weekend, which was about 3 months later, David and I went to a poetry slam at the Brooklyn Moon Cafe. I remember it because that was the day we shared our first kiss. The atmosphere was perfect and the energy that night was just what I loved about New York. While I was at school in Connecticut, I would come into the city and enjoy everything about it. So that night was magic; the city was so amazing and I thought David was so exotic because he had this New York accent. It was just an exciting night. We were walking back from the cafe and crossing this little bridge when he picked me up and spun me around and kissed me. It was wonderful. I remember those details about it and each other. I think that I try to say that we fell in love with that first kiss, but if I'm honest, I fell in love when I first saw him.

But that didn't mean that everything was perfect.

Even though I loved his New York accent, after we started dating, a real sticking point for me was his sarcastic New York "attitude," where he would say something that I thought was mean-spirited or sharp. I wasn't really sure that I could deal with it. I was on the verge of letting that be the reason I was about to let him go, but I mentioned it to my father, who quickly told me to calm my sensitive self down.

>> *David*

He always has such good advice.

>> *Jamillah*

He reminded me that a) I liked David a lot, which clearly was based on what I was sharing with him about David and b) that's just the way people are in New York City. My father made me realize that David's sarcasm wasn't about me. It was just the way David was.

Even though I believed it wasn't about me, in my heart, his sarcastic jokes still stung and I let him know, (repeatedly), that it was something he was going to have to work on. This was hard because for David making sarcastic comments came as naturally as flowers growing in the Spring. But not hurting my feelings was more important to him than getting a laugh, and getting a laugh is *very* important to him. In spite of this, he was willing to sacrifice his sarcasm for me. He's sweet like that. This helped me to take my own advice. Let go and get to know him better, more deeply. I was really using this one personality trait as a reason to try to abandon ship. I could feel us getting closer and maybe this was me focusing on something else so that I didn't have to pay attention to what I was feeling. The more that I looked at everything about him that I liked and loved, the less his sarcasm became an issue. I had given it less attention and oddly enough, it became less important.

What was, and continues to be, important is that this man wasn't some hard-edged man with a chip on his shoulder and a fight against the world. He was just a man who liked sarcastic jokes, but he never had any harsh intention. When I lightened up about it, I found that there were times when I could laugh with him and even hit him with a couple of jokes of my own. Being willing to sacrifice his sarcasm, which I know comes second nature to him, made me love him all the more.

Love Is Worth the Sacrifice *- Today, with publicized stories of couples walking away after only days of marriage and even more people living as though sacrifice is nearly a curse word, we say: It's worth the sacrifice. For us sacrifice means that we are willing to give up something that we thought was valuable or important for something more important: Love and our Happiness.*

SHE SAYS:
"BE WILLING TO BE EXPOSED"

The surprising thing is when you are really ready to be in love, you can be open—but shut down at the same time. I was in love and I knew it, but I thought love was supposed to look and feel a specific way. And when my preconceptions of love did not materialize, I thought I had a reason to bolt. But thank goodness I never ran. I was in love, but I still had moments of resistance. I realize that my fear only surfaced so that it could be swept away. I knew that David was the man for me because all of the work that I needed to do on myself (like being more patient and not being so defensive) I was willing to do in front of him, trusting that he would be there for me and not try to control the outcome. He let me be me.

» David

I remember that I started working at the Low Income Investment Fund on John Street, in Lower Manhattan (near where the Twin Towers stood) on Tuesday, March 2nd. I remember that fact because few people start a new job on a Tuesday, but I had something to do that Monday. Most of all I remember it was March 2nd because as it would turn out, my first day of work was also Jamillah's birthday. I had no idea at that time, of course. But it's a fact that we always remember as important and impactful. It was a sign that we were meant to be together. We just didn't know it.

Love at first sight may sound like something from a movie, but in our case it was more real than anything I've ever watched on screen. While I was walking down the hall in the office during that first week, I saw a photo on the wall of a staff retreat from the year before. I noticed this beautiful woman with a great smile and a nice figure (I'm just saying) and I remember saying to myself, "Something tells me that I'm going to marry that girl." I had never met her (she was on the west coast) but I remember telling my friend Tracy Grant about it because I just had a feeling.

A month later when our office flew out to San Francisco for the annual retreat, I had already decided it was a done deal. She was mine—I just didn't know how yet. I had told NO ONE at work about this, because even I knew I might be tripping.

When we arrived at the company's California headquarters, I noticed her in her office, chewing on the end of a pen, furiously punching her calculator and looking very intense. As soon as I saw this my class insecurities kicked in, and I thought, "That's it, she's just too 'bourgie' for me." (This was a common escape hatch I'd used to put the brakes on any potential relationship before it went anywhere.) What I didn't realize was that two of my co-workers (Valerie and Lisa) had already decided that Jamillah and I would be a good couple. So they kept dropping hints to me about her, like I hadn't already noticed. I'd noticed Jamillah (long before we'd gotten there).

I remember the restaurant we went to that night being either Cambodian or Malaysian. I hadn't had a chance to make any moves, but I noticed where Jamillah was sitting and I had to bump Valerie out of the way. Valerie was probably just trying to sit close to her so that she could bring me some more information, but I was ready to make my move.

I took the seat and started getting to know her myself. When the people from California went to go out dancing that night, I had to say no because I was exhausted (and I was kicking myself) but I was tired and I had to be at the airport early in the morning.

In an act of divine intervention (at least I'd like to think so) the company decided to send me back out to San Francisco not more than a month later. The company flying someone back out so soon was not only unusual, it was unprecedented. But hey, I was happy. Jamillah and I got to spend more time together. But I still didn't make my move. I told myself I needed to be sure.

What I was sure of was that I had fallen hard and I think I just needed to make sure I was dealing with a heart issue and not just a physical thing. I knew it was my heart, but I wasn't used to feeling like that so I had to take my time, in my mind. That's what I was telling myself, but the truth is I already knew.

While I was in California, Jamillah told me she was going to be coming back to New Jersey to see her family and I used that to justify waiting. I think I didn't make a move because I really just wanted to seal the deal on my turf. Besides, when I was with her in California, she took me to see this beach that to get to we had to drive through mountain cliffsides! We don't have mountains in NYC.

Jamillah was enamored with the views and wanted me to see how majestic they were. All I could think was, "Is she trying to kill me?" (I told you I was suspicious) "Keep your eyes on the road!"

I felt out of my element; my mojo felt off. As we drove along the edge of a twisting mountainside with no lights on the road I was so scared that I couldn't enjoy the view and she was upset because she wanted to share California's beauty with me. It was the first time I heard her say, "You're making me soooo mad," with her voice rising to the cutest pitch. It used to be one of her favorite subconscious expressions, but she stopped saying it because I always made fun of it later on. But that was the first time I'd heard it.

Anyway, I knew I would be in my element in my city and New York has a way of being a character in whatever story you are telling. So, I think I waited because I wanted her to be with me, in my space. I knew that if I felt the attraction as strongly in New York as I felt it when I saw her in California, then she was the one. (But I knew that already. I just wanted to be sure.)

Six weeks later she was in NYC, and I wanted to show her around town. I remember walking her into a bookstore in Brooklyn. I tried to act smooth as I handed her a copy of my book, *Do Platanos Go Wit' Collard Greens?* I was trying to impress her and it worked.

» *Jamillah*
He was smooth, I'll give him that.

» *David*

If you don't want to just be friends, make your move before you are **permanently put in the "FRIEND" camp.** I have witnessed this happen to so many guys. It ain't pretty.
David

But I also knew that if I didn't make my move on this visit, I was going to be put into the permanent "friend" camp. I didn't want her to be my friend; I wanted her to be my girl. More than my girl, she was *the* woman. As we strolled through Brooklyn after going to a poetry slam, I put my right arm around her. I remember the blue skirt and white top that she had on that night. I picked her up and kissed her. She thought it was bold. But I had to do what I had to do.

I met her family during that visit and one memory stands out crystal clear to this day. She asked her grandmother, "Is he the one?" I tried to be cool about it, but I was thinking it was too soon for the question, even though I had already answered it for myself.

» *Jamillah*

I don't even remember asking. And I can't believe I said it in front of him! I'm so embarrassed. But I had to ask, because a few months before my grandmother had called me and said that I would meet "the one" before May.

David

When her grandmother said yes, it made me feel good. Later that week, I seriously thought about asking her to marry me, but I thought that the age difference between me and her grandmother was too great ☺.

» *Jamillah*

I told you, sarcastic.

» *David*

Seriously though, I thought that Jamillah would think I was crazy since we had literally just started dating.

Not long after, though, I thought she might be crazy. One of the things she used to do a lot, especially early on, was cry. I thought something was wrong with her because she would cry so much. Like *Cry Me A River* cry!

» *Jamillah*

It's true. It's one of those things he let me work on in front of him.

Signs

There are all kinds of signs. There are Stop signs. There are Yield signs. And there are signs that say "He should have seen that coming!" Like when Mayor Marion Barry got busted with crack in a motel. You're the mayor of Washington, D.C.! The Capital! He thought he could get away with that, but he really should have seen that coming! Then there are the Aha Signs. When the light bulb suddenly goes off and you say, "Damn, that's a good idea!" You never know when these signs will appear, but you need to be open to them in life, in romance, and in business.

When I think about it, my idea for the play really came from a sign. *In my last semester of college, I was selected to participate in the New York State Legislative Intern Program in Albany, NY. As interns, we were randomly assigned to work in the office of a State Assemblyperson. I was assigned to work in the office of Jose' Serrano (who is now a Congressman from the South Bronx).*

I remember that day clearly, because it was such a coincidence! I was nervous and excited when I met him. I said "I'm David Lamb, from Astoria, Queens, Astoria Projects." And he looked at me with a strange, almost "suspicious" look on his face. And I'm thinking, "What the hell is going on? What did I just say?" **Finally, he says, "Lamb? Astoria? When I moved to this country from Puerto Rico, the first person I met was Ricky Lamb."** *I said, "Yeah, that's my uncle." We were both shocked because they hadn't spoken or seen each other since seventh grade.*

That got me to thinking about my own life, and how long Black and Latino communities had been intimately integrated in New York City, and influenced each other spanning decades and across generations. I decided that I wanted to write a story about it, from Latin Jazz to Mambo to Hip Hop - Platanos Y Collard Greens, a story that makes people laugh, makes them reminisce, and leaves them feeling inspired. **David**

» *David*

I didn't know she was that sensitive and I didn't know what it felt like for her to be this close with someone—but I thought she cried too much. Given the remarkably ridiculous reasons I had ended relationships before, I realized that she was the one when I noticed her crying and even said something about it, maybe even cracked a joke about how much she cried, but I never thought about leaving. She was the one. It was destiny.

HE SAYS:
"SOMETIMES COINCIDENCES ARE SIGNS"

Remember that Mel Gibson movie *Signs*? All of the coincidences and hints, and well signs, come together at the end showing that all along the characters were being pointed in certain directions. Sometimes that happens in life. I mean really, Jamillah's grandmother has a dream that she's going to meet "the one" and I show up!

» *Jamillah*

I'm just glad he didn't turn out to be some psycho.

» *David*

Me, too. But there were always signs that we were meant to be together.

Not only did I start to work at the job where we met on her birthday, but it turned out there were a few other signs. During the summer after my first year of graduate school at Princeton, I worked at a bank in the same neighborhood where Jamillah grew up and still lived. (I like to think that she saw me there and started stalking me then.) You have to understand; I'm a

New Yorker, to the bone, that means that for me New York is the Center of the Universe. For me to go to another city to work was unfathomable. Yet there I was on the South Side of Chicago working at the bank in her neighborhood, where her family banked!

A few years later, I published *Do Platanos Go Wit' Collard Greens?* And I toured colleges giving lectures and readings. One of the first schools I visited was Amherst College, and one of the students who hosted the reading and who introduced me before I spoke was Jamillah's brother. (At the time he didn't know me from a can of paint—and today he's my brother-in-law!) I'm always amazed by that. Not long after that I spoke at Seton Hall University in New Jersey, and one of the students involved in bringing me to campus was her cousin. Years later when I found this out, I said that her family had been setting us up for years.

HE SAYS:
"MEN ALL PAUSE...AND PAY ATTENTION"

While I was already certain about how I felt, looking back, I can't ignore the signs. I also can't believe that I remember so many details, but I do and I think it's a great thing. Yes, we notice skirts and tears and conversations with grandmothers. Men don't get permission to be sentimental, but we are (just in different ways). Women will remember what they were wearing only if they felt beautiful in it, but men remember that you were beautiful (and remember the outfit as part of those details). Don't dismiss the skirt if you didn't like it or the day just because you weren't feeling your best. Just like you want your man to find certain components of your relationship significant, there are details that he remembers, too. Don't be so quick to count him out as not vested in you because he doesn't recall everything you do. There are certain things you do, and you were doing, when he was watching and paying attention that he can repeat and respond to in moments when you think he didn't notice.

We notice.

Fighting Over Memories

Some memories are those we've created together, and others are nostalgic memories from before we ever knew the other existed. They are all important, but sometimes they can cause fights that at the time seem so serious, but later seem so silly.

Keep this in mind when you are itching to toss out an old, raggedy T-shirt that you both know he shouldn't be wearing anymore because all you can see is that it's full of holes. For him it's full of memories; it was the shirt he was wearing when he won his last high school football game. Remember that when you're wondering why her prom dress is still taking up room in the closet.

» *David*

Nerd moment:
I have been collecting comics since I was in junior high school. (Of course this wasn't something I broadcast to Jamillah when we first started dating.)

» *Jamillah*

Luckily, all of my brothers are *Star Wars* fanatics, so I was used to the condition.

» *David*

As my comic collection continued to grow, it began to invade and colonize a portion of our bedroom and beyond. Jamillah's normally sweet demeanor turned sour and she launched a cleaning rampage.

» *Jamillah*

His comics were out of control!

» *David*

Of course I resisted, claiming that I was just about to read comics I hadn't touched in years. We were at a stalemate between my memories and her need for organization and neatness as opposed to my (like 95 percent of the men I know) comfort with disorganized chaos. At first, she issued an ultimatum that would have rendered my collection to the recyclables trash bin.

However, without me knowing, she put on her "organization thinking cap", and within a couple of days, via the internet, comic organizing bins had arrived. I was given my marching orders and a short time later, the comics were all stored in bins under *my* side of the bed—easy access for me, and out of her sight. After that, all of my questions about why she needed so many pairs of shoes went out the window.

» *Jamillah*

Sometimes relationships get off-track fighting over things that seem silly, but it happens all the time. And sometimes it's because it's not the possessions we are fighting over so much as the memories that are attached to them.

After our wedding, one of the biggest battles we had was over whose rug we would keep in the living room—his or mine. Of course, he thought his rug was nicer (New Yorkers never stop).

» *David*

But my rug was nicer.

» Jamillah

I have to admit it was—but that was beside the point. My rug was full of memories that I wasn't letting go of so easily. When he saw how much it meant to me, he agreed that we would keep my rug. (The truth was that I thought his rug was nicer, but for years, until our little girl came along, we had two rugs even though we only had room for one).

Sometimes my rug would stand upright in the hallway, sometimes it would be in our bedroom. Eventually we put it in the second bedroom that we'd turned into an office. However, when I was pregnant, and we were turning the second room into a bedroom for our daughter, I knew that we, all three of us, were going to be making new memories together and it was time to let my old rug go.

Besides, David and I have been creating more beautiful memories together.

David Visiting Jamillah in California -
See how tightly he's holding onto the rail!

Jamillah Visiting David in Brooklyn.

Jamillah and David in Chicago.

Jamillah with her Grandmother Shirlee "Hunabuna" Conway 1989.

OUR KEY INGREDIENT

Memories Matter

1 Cup of Making Room for New Memories

1 Tablespoon of Letting Go of Old Attachments

You may not remember the same thing; you may not even remember the same event the same way. Instead of spending so much energy trying to determine who was right or whose memories are more sentimental or matter more, try this on for size: *You are both right.*

Just as two people can never really remember the same thing exactly the same way, nor will the memories of what's important to you always be as important to the other person. What matters is that you allow yourself, and each other, the space to build new and better memories.

When you find yourself nit-picking about issues that you might be willing to draw swords over, take the time to remember that you're not in a competition. Breathe and smile and let your partner tell their version of the story. And if you don't remember or don't agree, don't freak out—reach out. Listen and let your honey tell you the story the way they remember it. You may learn something important about yourself that you didn't realize they noticed. You may also discover something new about your partner.

Memories

COOKING WITH LOVE

Some Tips for Cooking Up
Loving Memories that Matter:

1. Write a love letter to each other describing your first date.

2. Plan a surprise date for your partner.

3. Tell each other a joke.

4. Text your partner the top three things that you love about them.

5. Do something together that you don't normally do, like play a board game, or watch one of his/her favorite TV shows with him/her. (Really be interested in the characters, plot or play-by-play action).

6. Make a CD or MP3 playlist of his/her five songs that most describe your love for each other.

7. Discover something new together that neither of you have ever done; visit a museum, garden, zoo, or drive to a different town for dinner.

8. Dance together in the living room, with just the two of you doing the craziest dances you can.

9. Take a class together, like yoga, kickboxing, painting, or cooking.

10. Go to an event together, like a concert or play. (We've heard *Platanos Y Collard Greens* is pretty good).

END OF CHAPTER PLAYLIST

Chapter Two – Vision of Love

1. **Vision of Love** by Mariah Carey

2. **I Found That Girl** by The Jackson 5

3. **I Need to Know** by Marc Anthony

4. **Can't Take My Eyes Off Of You** by Lauryn Hill

5. **Hope That We Can Be Together Soon** by Sharon Paige & Harold Melvin and the Blue Notes

Just The Two of Us

❧

As we mentioned in the opening chapter, there are so many ways that couples are and can be in "business" together. In fact, some of the major tasks in your life can at times require a level of planning, organization and execution that mirrors running an actual business. For us, our first "business" venture was planning our wedding.

Sometimes You Just Dive Right In!

» Jamillah

People are continually amazed when they hear that I didn't have any major considerations about going into business with my husband. None. But there was a reason for that: Our wedding.

» David

I should have known that Jamillah wanted to be an event planner from the moment she began planning our wedding. And I should have known that being a theater producer would come just as naturally for her. Looking back, it's clear that our wedding was our first production. The only thing that stopped her from turning it into a $100 million dollar epic was our budget.

» Jamillah

I did a great job. Do you know how much weddings cost!

» David

She scouted locations up and down the east coast trying to find the perfect venue to accommodate her very large extended family and my tiny family. She auditioned and hired talent, technical crew, staff and catering. She made sure that everyone and everything was taken care of and that all the bills were paid. And she made sure that we started on time—not taking into account that she was an hour late.

» Jamillah

Because your cousin got lost driving me to the venue, which was only five minutes away!

» David

True.

» Jamillah

He is right, though; it was our first production. From the beginning, I should have known we were destined to do something on stage because at the end of our vows he surprised me by gently snatching the microphone and telling the band to "hit it!" Next thing I knew he's singing Taj Mahal's *Queen Bee*. I was crying tears of joy, for him to show such public love, knowing he can't sing a lick!

» *David*

Like a frog with the mumps. My boss said, "You must *really* love her!"

» *Jamillah*

When I look back at the photos, everyone was crying.

» *David*

But it was all love. The crazy thing is the night before, her girlfriend drove her to my apartment to get our wedding rings because Jamillah was afraid I would lose or forget them and show up to the ceremony with no rings. And I had mistakenly left the ring box on top of the song lyrics where she might have seen them. I'm thankful she didn't.

Quitting My Job

» *Jamillah*

When we first decided to turn David's book into a play, I thought it would be a great "thing-to-do" for a couple of week-ends. At the time I was working as a Vice-President at Citibank, so I saw this as a venture and maybe even an adventure. I saw this as right up my alley. I got to organize the details, work on all of the moving parts and make sure that things were in their respective places. It was about organization and that's a big deal for me. I was also really excited about seeing David take this major leap of faith. I knew that college groups around the country had been encouraging him to turn it into a play. So, to me, it was a natural next step. I was just glad that I had the talents to be able to help turn the vision up a notch.

I didn't even think about the play as us being in business together until I walked into my boss' office at the bank and quit my job. It wasn't a whim. I had thought about it. The play had been going well for two years and I wanted to give it my full attention. But if there was ever a moment when I thought "What am I doing?" that was it.

» David

That's what I was thinking!

» Jamillah

Who walks away from the comfort of a corporate job?

» David

Exactly. Who walks away from the comfort of a corporate job!

» Jamillah

This move was the opposite of how I had been prepared for life as the responsible young lady who was told to "choose a proper career." I had done that and I had succeeded. So I think that some part of me was really hungry for this adventure. I thought about working part-time to keep income coming into the house...

» David

I was really pushing the part-time thing.

» *Jamillah*

But I thought more about my need to commit myself to this work and wanted to help my husband build his dream, which I believed in. I didn't learn until recently that he was really adamant that I should have stayed at the bank, at least part-time. At the time, we were both reading the book, *Rich Dad, Poor Dad*, and the author had stressed "keep your job and work your business." All I know is that I wanted to support him and I believed in the vision. Besides, I was really stressed at the bank. I knew that leaving would also be stressful, but it would be a different kind of stress. So I took the plunge.

» *David*

I guess this was one of those *Men Are From Mars, Women Are From Venus* moments. In my mind, I was being clear and adamant. But the truth is I, like of lot of men I know, often think I'm being clear and adamant when I'm actually being unclear and passive; waiting, expecting her to read my mind, then having an attitude when she doesn't. My mother had been trying to break me of this idea that people should be able to read my mind since I was a little boy.

Well, men, I hate to break it to you but SHE CANNOT READ YOUR MIND. Stop it and admit that it's not them, it's us. It's our fear of expressing our true wants and needs. David

» *Jamillah*

Even today, sometimes he'll stare at me waiting for me to read his mind! And I'm like, "Boy if you don't stop it."

» *David*

I find that a lot of men believe women should be able to read our minds and fulfill our wants and needs without us having to say anything.

(Just be the 'strong, silent type'). I know that it happens to me, and I have to keep working on it. After all, I'm in the business of communicating ideas, and sometimes I even expect the actors to read my mind. It doesn't work there either.

» *Jamillah*

Yes, he's worked on it. Now that we were in business for ourselves, full- time, we had to figure out how to run this thing and reading his mind was not going to work.

Infinitely Perfectible

» *David*

In the movies once a film is shot and released, that's it. The actor's performance is permanently set in stone. In theater, however, each performance on stage is new, an opportunity to continually strive to produce great performances; to be fresh and discover something new—even a small hand movement by an actor can further perfect a scene. In short, theater is *infinitely perfectible* because it is alive and you can always search for new ways to make it better. I think that our belief and commitment to make theater infinitely perfectible is why so many people have come to see *Platanos* three and four times. Each time is fresh. And that's exactly how we approach our relationship. It's *infinitely perfectible*—fresh, alive, new.

People Do The Darndest Things:
We had an actor call us and say "I'm here on the train but I don't see anyone." Well maybe that's because he was on the train going to *Boston* when he knew damn well the show was in *Baltimore*.

Just as we discovered theater and relationships are infinitely perfectible, we have learned that we as individuals are as well. It definitely takes work—personal striving to better yourself to have a relationship that produces Love and Happiness. In our case, the added stress of running a business together, without the safety net of a job with a steady paycheck, meant that I had a lot of growing to do.

Neither as a lawyer nor a professor, jobs I'd had before going into theater, had I needed to manage people. This was a huge change.

As a manager of people, I've had to deal with everything, from relationships amongst cast members that spilled over into the production to being a big brother to an actor and helping them grow and find themselves onstage and off; from dealing with feelings of under-appreciation from others and myself to dealing with management issues so ridiculous that you didn't even have a rule for it, because you never could have imagined something so ridiculous, to finding ways to inspire others. I've had to do it all.

I learned quickly that to be in this business, and in the business called life, there were (and are) some tools that I needed to help guide me through the process. In all honesty, early on when difficulties arose, I found that we were bringing stress into the relationship, and I knew if we continued to allow it, we were going to be in trouble! I knew we needed to find resources to help us not get too high in the good times or too low when our best-laid plans didn't work out as we'd planned.

I've said before that I believe in signs, and one Sunday morning after a stressful Saturday at the theater, I got up extra early determined to feed our souls and find some help for our internal growth. I went to the website for Sufi Books (a bookstore I liked that was once in downtown Manhattan) and saw that later that day they were having a workshop with the author of *The Anger Diet*. It promoted exactly what we needed: 30 days to a less stressful life. The workshop was a blessing and gave me tools to cope with stress and anger.

After that, I also got over myself about my feelings of what people should do and how they should act, and began reading Dale Carnegie's books, *How To Win Friends and Influence People* and *How To Stop Worrying and Start Living*. I was quite pleasantly surprised to find Dr. Martin Luther King's *Strength To Love*, a collection of amazing sermons for anyone looking to grow up, be ready for love and take charge of their lives—and their business.

> *You've also got to be willing to build yourself up individually.*

Finding some of the tools that I needed among these books has been really helpful. In addition, resources we've used including couples yoga have helped to make sure that our work life doesn't unduly burden our home life. I knew it was necessary for me, as a husband, as a partner and as a man to find what I needed, so that I was dealing with my business as business and not as frustration. Having a partner who is a sounding board is a wonderful thing, but you've also got to be willing to build yourself up individually so that you are clear about your strengths and willing to find resources to help you where you are challenged by forces outside of, and in the natural course of, your life. All of it helps to keep the conversations at home in the right perspective and in their proper place.

It's amazing to think of now, but Jamillah is right, our wedding really was our first production. What we didn't realize at the time was that the strengths and weaknesses we entered into our relationship with were the same ones we had when we entered into business. Therefore, the work on ourselves that we had to do in our relationship to keep it loving, healthy and happy, we also had to do on ourselves in our business relationship, to help our heads not get too big on the sunny days and not hang too low when the storms hit. Being in business together and being together all the time forced us, and continues to prod us, to be better.

For the Love of Money...and Shoes

> **No Money, Mo' Problems**
>
> **David** — I work so that I can have mental security. I want to have a certain amount of money in the bank so that I don't have to worry. I remember being unemployed early in my career as an attorney and the insecurity it brought me.
>
> **Jamillah** — I work so that I can have the things money can buy: vacations, a nice home, cute clothes for our daughter, but I don't buy all the things I would if I were making all the financial decisions alone. If I did, David would be in intensive care.

» Jamillah

I had to learn to be better with and about money. My grandmother didn't mind spending at all and I must have inherited that trait from her. I love to shop, not excessively, but David thinks it can be at times. We have to have real talks about money and our family so that we don't butt heads about it. I am the one who ensures that all of the bills are paid in a timely manner. I am a *Queen Bee* about order and structure. And when I know that everything we have is secured and uncompromised, I spend. I spend with the assurance that I'm not overspending. But that's not the same as saving.

» *David*

I'm a saver.

» *Jamillah*

When we knew that we were in love and wanted to be together, we decided to buy an apartment together. The interesting part was that as the "logical" one, I am the one who had been diligent about making sure that my credit rating was strong, so that I would always be able to buy whatever I wanted, when I was ready. The problem was I wasn't saving any money to make sure that when the time came I was really ready.

» *David*

That's a long, roundabout way of saying her pockets were empty.

» *Jamillah*

But I had great credit.

» *David*

Mine was not.

» *Jamillah*

When we decided to buy our first place, we would not have been able to get the mortgage without my excellent credit—but we would not have been able to purchase it without David, because he was the one who had actually saved the money to make the down payment.

It's that kind of balance—yin and yang, opposites attracting—that has given us what we need in order to co-exist in life and in business together. It's not just that we have each other's back; we know each other's strongest attributes and have done the work to be able to know who to let do what and when.

» *Jamillah*

Kaira Sojourner
*Our daughter's name **was a compromise**. I loved Sojourner Truth and what she stood for— a righteous, do good woman. I used to say "Every little Black girl in America should have Sojourner in their name somewhere. But Jamillah did not want Sojourner as our daughter's name. She thought it was too old timey. So we kept looking and I came across the name of a song from Mali, Kaira, which means peace and happiness. Well that struck a chord with both of us, and although I was still bent on Sojourner, I agreed to Kaira and Sojourner became her middle name.* **David**

David is much better at all of the creative aspects of the business. He deals with the actors (and the rehearsals), he deals with (most of the) casting and I manage the company's operation. We have conversations about what we feel strongly about, we make our points, we listen and if we don't agree, we try to reach a compromise. If it's an either or situation we go with the decision of the person who feels more strongly, because even if the decision turns out to be a mistake, we know it was not intentional, and that person had the best intentions for our family and the business. It's about knowing that we are in this together. In thinking about us, as a couple and a family, we hear each other out and compromise and we try to stay open to trying something new. We trust each other's opinions, and so we communicate on all aspects of life and business whether one person handles an item most of the time or not. We never say something is "not in your lane." Even where we know the other is strong, we bounce ideas off of each other because we respect each other—and regard each other's opinion as something that matters.

We All Want To Be Appreciated

Brooklyn

*Living in Brooklyn **was a compromise**. I had always loved New York City, but actually living here was a different story. I have dreams of a home with a backyard and a driveway. I wanted to move to New Jersey and David wanted to stay in Brooklyn. I decided to compromise because I realized that I had moved all around the country and could adapt to almost any situation. For David, moving would be a major upheaval, because he had lived in New York City his whole life. So I agreed that we would live in Brooklyn and revisit the conversation after we had children. **Jamillah***

One of the biggest keys we've discovered about successfully being in business together is also one of the keys to being in a loving relationship together—MUTUAL APPRECIATION. Even when one of us takes on a project because we do it well or it's natural to us, we've learned to take the time and acknowledge the work by expressing appreciation. The simplest gesture or sign of appreciation can go a long way to help your significant other feel like they are making a significant contribution to your life, your family or your business.

» *Jamillah*

It's been amazing to be in business together, but as we go forward, I think it's going to be really important to carve out non-business time. Because we are always together, we are always thinking about the business. We aren't always doing business, but in the middle of the night, David may jump up and want to discuss an idea or we'll be at home and he'll want to talk about something business-related and I'm thinking about groceries or the fact that there are dirty dishes in the sink! Who can think with dirty dishes in the sink! I can't think with dirty dishes in the sink.

» *David*

I can.

» *Jamillah*

We have been talking about how we need to carve out actual, factual non-business time. So we're working on it.

Balance *— You can never take for granted that seeing each other is the same as spending time together. You've got to find places to go and pockets of time where you just get to be a couple, even when the kids arrive and the family grows.*

It's about balance and finding a way to make sure that the "us" of being a couple stays central to the "why" of everything that we do. We work well in business together because we work so well in life together. To us, it's okay to say "I need more of you" even when you see each other often. After all, when you first came together, you dated. That dating aspect is the hook. It keeps you thinking of ways to discover more about each other, to please each other and to take each other away from the blahs and the blows of life. The key is to find the time to stop and breathe.

SHE SAYS:
"IT'S ABOUT THE TEAM"

Our love is a business. Our family is a business. Our business is a joy because we love doing what we do, together. We also know how to step back and let each other shine, and step up and support each other where it's necessary.

What's For Dinner?

At our wedding, my Matron of Honor, Ru, said "to all of you who bought pots and pans as wedding gifts, you might as well take them back, because Jamillah is not cooking." It's true. Mostly my meals consisted of warming up frozen peas and chicken fingers and I was not opposed to cereal for dinner.

Once we had our daughter that changed. We could no longer have a refrigerator that was only full of condiments. So I bought some cookbooks and I started cooking. I kept it exciting by trying a new recipe each night, so it didn't feel like drudgery. And David took on the task of cooking breakfast (he makes the best omelets) and baking enough chicken on Sunday to last three or four nights.

We changed our eating habits (and lowered our take out bills) together. Neither of us feels put upon because we both know that the other is willing to step up and get done what needs to be done for our family. **Jamillah**

We went into business when we decided to be a couple. We were already making decisions about going on vacations and making other life choices that involved the family, so going into business together was about being able to find balance, continuing to trust, respect and rely on each other. Thankfully, we communicated well even before we ventured into business together.

HE SAYS:
"FRIENDS CAN BE LOVERS AND
BUSINESS PARTNERS, TOO."

When you are with someone whom you cherish as your friend, it's easy to rest on their shoulders and trust their opinions in the decision-making process. That's what we do in business because that's what we were doing in our relationship. We celebrate each other's strengths, and know how to communicate when, and if, we feel like we aren't being appreciated. It's about being able to see it and say it. We don't let things get too deep or too far off course because we would rather spend our energy on being happy rather than on getting things back on track. And who wants to watch the car you've built and polished go off into a ditch anyway?

1. David and Jamillah speaking before NYC High School Teachers.
Photo: Benjamin Chambers

2. Platanos cast members with the hilarious Charlamagne (center) radio host from New York City's POWER 105.1FM's popular morning show, "The Breakfast Club". (left to right) Sofia, Mera, Krystal, Jocelyn, Gordon, Preston and Hjordy's

4. Dynamic radio host Jeff Foxx (left) from New York City's 107.5 WBLS with David Lamb

Behind the Scenes

3. The charismatic host of "Kissing After Dark with Lenny", Lenny Green (center) with Platanos cast members (left to right) Toi, Leon, Ohene, Mera, and Edgar (kneeling)

5. Mayor Wayne Smith of Irvington, NJ (right) awarding a Proclamation to David and Jamillah Lamb

6. US Congressman Gregory W. Meeks (left) and US Congressman Donald M. Payne (right) speaking before Congressional Black Caucus Members attending Platanos Y Collard Greens performance.
Photo: Kewulay Kamara

7. City of Newark Council President Donald M. Payne Jr. (right) awarding a Proclamation to Jamillah and David Lamb

8. Jamillah Lamb with the multitalented Egypt Sherrod (right) host of HGTV's "Property Virgins" and "Middays with Egypt" on New York City's 107.5 WBLS

OUR KEY INGREDIENT:

It's About Balance

2 Heaping Cups of Appreciation
1 Cup of Self-Knowledge
1 Cup of Modesty
1 Cup of Trust

So many times we worry about not wanting to be sexist or about being politically incorrect inside our own relationships that we don't just let people do what they do best.

We know people who have burnt many a chicken or hung many a crooked picture because the world makes you think that you have to have parity in every way, every minute of every day. So many couples think that they have to divide everything in half, when what we are all looking for, in love and in life, is balance.

If you are better suited to handling the finances or cooking the meals, man or woman, do that because it's best for your household. Don't care about what other people think. Know what you do well and be willing to celebrate each other. Don't cook if you know you can't (because we all know that the only thing busy people know how to make are reservations). Make dinner reservations one night a week and treat the one who is always cooking to a night out. If your partner does administrative tasks at a desk all day, then the other partner can take a massage class so that you can soothe that neck tension after the checks are in the mail.

When it's about balance, there are contributions from both sides that are respected. When you reach that kind of equilibrium everyone gets what they deserve—APPRECIATION.

Appreciation

COOKING WITH LOVE

Season Your Relationship with Love and Happiness:

1. Put your money (and your energy) where your mouth is. Be willing to invest in your family and yourself.

2. Be patient with each other (and with yourself). We've all got things to learn. Learn them and use them to better yourself.

3. Let your partner do what they do well. Harmony and balance are better than parity.

4. Learn to manage expectations (of yourself and others).

5. Be your partner's biggest cheerleader, because when they feel appreciated, they appreciate you and your partnership thrives.

END OF CHAPTER PLAYLIST

▶

Chapter Three — Just The Two of Us

1. **Just The Two of Us** by Grover Washington Jr. with Bill Withers

2. **Queen Bee** by Taj Mahal

3. **Los Amantes (The Lovers)** by Susana Baca

4. **It Feels Good** by Tony Toni Tone'

5. **It Takes Two (To Make a Thing Go Right)** by Rob Base and DJ EZ Roc

CHAPTER FOUR

Unbreakable

DISAGREE WITHOUT BEING ... DISAGREEABLE –
Dr. Martin Luther King, Jr.

ome couples love to fight. They think it evokes passion and speaks to the depths of their connection to each other.

Some couples hate to fight. They think it reflects disharmony in their connection or means that something is wrong with their relationship.

Love them or hate them, understand them or avoid them, disagreements will occur. So how have we, and how do we, continue to run a business together, 24/7, without killing each other? We had to learn to disagree without being disagreeable. Being in business together made learning how to handle disagreements a necessity. The funny thing is everything started out so smoothly we had no idea this was a lesson we were going to have to learn.

» David

The first night of the show was June 27, 2003. We had been married for a year. We had hired my roommate from grad school and law school, Summerhill 7, as the director. Although we rented a small theater right in the heart of Broadway, don't get it twisted, this was still a low-budget, do-it-yourself space. Jamillah and I had to clean the bathrooms. We had to clean the theater before and after the show. And that night, opening night, right before the audience was to take their seats, we had a rodent visitor stroll across the stage and take a bow like he'd put on the performance of his life and gotten a standing ovation. Of course, this made us nervous about going ahead, but it was a sold-out performance. Everyone was filled with excitement and nervous energy. We were too nervous to even go into the theater. I stood outside the door and waited for the first laugh. I still remember that first laugh, which, for a writer is always thrilling. I remember that they laughed again and then again and they kept on laughing, louder and louder each time.

» Jamillah

I remember that first night like it was yesterday. I was so nervous! I couldn't watch the show ☺. I was too excited. Besides, we hadn't reserved any seats for ourselves and there was nowhere for us to sit or even stand. So I listened at the door. Every time they laughed, I got goose bumps. I remember this guy running out during intermission; he couldn't wait to get on his cell phone and tell his friend that he had to come and see the play.

» David

The last thing we expected when we began this journey together was that six years later a team of undercover national security officers would be doing a security sweep of the theater before we could seat the audience, but that was exactly what happened when thirty members of the Congressional Black Caucus came to see the play. These congressmen and congresswomen from across the country were there to see our play! How could I not be proud? Regardless of what had transpired in my life, in my mind I was just a kid from the projects.

What we've learned is **the reasons why and the ways in which we fight can determine if a couple can make it through the night** *(or through the fight) to keep loving each other, and move on to the rest of their life and their love together.*

» *Jamillah*

I remember once early in our marriage I was mad at David about something and I called a girlfriend of mine to vent. She laughed because to her, it seemed so minor. I'd called her really upset because I'd thought that we had just had a big fight. When she asked me to describe some of our other "fights", she really started laughing, because David and I didn't actually have what most people would consider fights. But that was before we went into business together.

» *David*

Jamillah is right. We didn't fight—until we went into business together. And if I'm being absolutely honest, not really <u>until my pride was on the line</u>. More to the point, as long as things were going well on the business end, we didn't fight. But if there were any hiccups or if we were being affected by the Great Recession (and let's face it everyone, well 99% of us, has been affected) then I would look for someone to blame. My two favorite targets were myself and my wife, in that order.

I was looking to blame someone for a decision that at the time seemed like the right thing to do. And in our business there could be a hundred decisions a day, everything from casting, to selecting a theater, from scheduling shows to selecting lighting; from setting ticket prices to choosing which radio or TV station to advertise on, and how much to spend on advertising. Casting blame and fighting were the easy things to do when I was having a hard time juggling those decisions. Maturing out of the blame game took me some time.

» Jamillah

One of the things we've learned is that we not only have to be friends with each other, we have to be friends with ourselves.

We're glad that we are friends in our marriage. We are each other's great cheerleader and support system. But one of the things we've learned is that we not only have to be friends with each other, we have to be friends with ourselves. Let me repeat: We each had to learn to treat ourselves like a friend. That means the same support, patience and encouragement that we would give a good friend, we still have to learn to give ourselves. Both David and I, and David especially, and **most people we know are excessively, and in some cases obsessively self-critical, which really is a form of self-abuse.** Think of all the times we as people belittle ourselves and tell ourselves that we're stupid because a decision we made didn't turn out quite like we'd planned or imagined it would. **Now ask yourself, would you treat a friend that way?**

» David

I remember one time when Jamillah had worked very hard to obtain the opportunity for us to perform an excerpt of the show at a multicultural conference. But when we got there, it didn't seem too multicultural to us, and they really didn't seem too interested in being exposed to anything multicultural.

» Jamillah

I had worked hard, planned hard, we had spent hard-earned money, but my plans didn't work out the way that I'd planned. That night in the hotel, I was beating myself up and berating myself, wondering how I could have been so stupid.

» David

And I started thinking, "Hey wait a minute that's my job—to beat myself up, so you can't be beating yourself up." I started laughing. But really, I was just trying to make her see that it wasn't the catastrophe she was making it out to be.

If we are perpetually judgmental of ourselves, how long will it be before we are judgmental of the one we love? How can we even offer love if we are spending so much time beating ourselves up?

» Jamillah

That was a rough one, because I'd had such high expectations.

Being in business was forcing us to learn, for our own sanity, not to get too high when times are good, or too low when our plans didn't quite work out the way we planned.

» David

Being in business was forcing us to learn, for our own sanity, not to get too high when times are good, or too low when our plans didn't quite work. This is really something that I have struggled with because my ego didn't (and sometimes still doesn't) allow for the possibility that something could turn out differently (especially a decision that could adversely affect my family). So if I planned something and it didn't quite work out the way I expected, no matter how small or truly insignificant, I would judge myself harshly.

HUMILITY IS NOT SO MUCH A VIRTUE, AS A NECESSITY IN ORDER TO LEARN - Idries Shah

I know so many guys who feel unworthy to be in a relationship when they are in the midst of beating themselves up. And then there are other guys I know who mess up the relationships they are in when they are riding high, feeling that their life is on the upswing, and they want to "trade up" or play the field. I see it as two sides of the same coin, really, either being too low on themselves or having too big a head.

As Jamillah mentioned, we really didn't fight until we went into business together. And we really didn't fight until a problem arose in business and I wanted to push blame on to her. I knew it was immature, but I had to grow out of it. Once I did, things that seemed hard became easier. Heavy burdens became light, momentary distractions, and we learned to handle disagreements like adults.

With that in mind, we've learned to disagree accordingly. That means that we learned to trust that we're going to land in a place where we can still look at each other and know that we are on each other's side. References to parents and pasts don't get thrown around like a football on a practice field. We don't hurl bombs into everyday conversations about who is supposed to do what in the kitchen or at work.

"You should've" this or "how come you don't"
has the potential of making your relationship feel
like something that can never be fulfilled, and it
dismisses all of the highs and harmony that you
know are the reason you are together.

» Jamillah

When we fight, we are clear that we are trying to clear up a misunderstanding between us or attempting to communicate a point. We don't spend a lot of time or energy disagreeing on the things that we wish the other would do because we are clear about who we are and so we don't expend effort trying to "should" each other. That can kill a relationship.

Sure, we fight (as in disagree), but we try never to really fight (as in go to war). Contrary to comedians and romance novels, love and war don't last long in the same story.

Sometimes, You Hit A Nerve

» *Jamillah*

When you are constantly up close and personal with someone —or something—it can be easy to not appreciate what is beautiful. As with anything that you are closest to, it is often the hardest thing to notice.

My husband has the most amazing relationship with our daughter. He is the sun and moon to her, literally. He puts her to bed and she often calls out for "Daddy" when she wakes up—whether it is 3 a.m. or 6 a.m. Even when I have been the one to stay up with her, she will still call out for her daddy to lull her to sleep. It was clearly a "David" thing and we understood that. What I didn't understand, however, was how much he felt drained by always being the one who got called. I would try to stay up with her as long as possible, but I'm a sleepyhead. I have been known to drift off to sleep at the drop of a hat.

One night, David clearly had had enough because when he addressed the "I can't believe you fell asleep" moment, he wasn't being his natural self. This time, it really stung with a tone that sounded like a) he felt I had fallen asleep on purpose and b) like he really believed that I was intentional in leaving him alone to handle this particular task. It hurt. My husband was questioning my intention and that dug right under my skin and hit nerve endings. It hurt that he actually thought that I was that selfish and meant to leave him to handle this alone. I had a moment where I thought to myself "What do you think about me?"

Where it really got to me was that I could feel the truth in his statement. I rely on my husband for certain things, but I didn't realize that I made them feel like expectations. And, I surely didn't realize that I was tapping into a place where he felt unappreciated, where he felt taken for granted as a person. I don't ever want him to think that. My mother laughingly said to me once, "You could never be a single parent", which is true because my husband and I clearly and evenly co-parent, as do many parents with hectic work lives and schedules.

My husband is a rock for me. I trust him and I try not to take advantage of the obvious fact that he is the kind of partner a wife can truly rely on. But I am also clear that there are things that I do that are simply a natural part of how we operate in our family. He doesn't pay attention to details in the house—I shop, I pay bills and make sure that tasks are completed—so there is balance. We jump in and handle what needs to be done, and in our own way. But where we can, we stay aware of being supports for each other. So I try to stay up with our daughter, droopy, heavy eyes and all, so that he doesn't think I expect him to do it or that it's his "job." He's just better at it.

» David

I really didn't know that she was wondering what I thought of her as a person. For me it wasn't that deep. What I was annoyed about was that my little girl, who I love to death, was a night owl and would never take her little behind to bed. And I had to stay up with her, get up in the middle of the night with her, and get up in the morning with her—and I was getting no props. But for Jamillah, it was as if I was questioning her integrity as a human being and a mother, but I was just talking about our little girl wearing me out. When we have a disagreement, I think that men keep it on topic, but sometimes women tend bring other aspects into it.

SHE SAYS:

"STAY ON SUBJECT"

When women fight, we can come from an arsenal of past pain that's still unresolved. We can have flashback moments where we are talking to old boyfriends and forgotten fathers, which means that we can often get nowhere near the actual point of the present disagreement.

That's not to suggest that sometimes we aren't really just upset about the socks being left all over the house, and the fight really is about leaving the socks all over the house. Because that happens!

But sometimes, the zings and stings of our disagreements are loaded down with history that needs to be put in perspective and left behind. It's really important to try and stay on subject—so that we don't bring up something that we declared off-limits or forgiven.

When you remember what you're fighting about, you can be clearer about getting to the thing that you're fighting for.

HE SAYS:
"SOME THINGS ARE NOT
WORTH THE FIGHT"

There are things that are worth fighting for, if you will, but never to the point that your heavy artillery blows a hole right through your partner's heart and soul. Even in a disagreement, Jamillah and I try to do no harm that cannot be undone. As I mentioned earlier *Love Is Not War*. When we disagree, we are careful about the words we choose and about how they shoot out of our mouths. We don't want to leave any emotionally dead bodies. And when it's done, we laugh, and remember that we're best friends.

David and Jamillah in Senegal West Africa 2004

OUR KEY INGREDIENT

✿

Lighten Up And Live
In The Moment!

*1 Cup of Friendship with
Yourself*

*1 Cup of Friendship with
Each Other*

Cool down about always trying to be right and feeling like you never get heard or bringing up things that have to do with your past. Be here. Now. In this relationship. Listen to what actually needs work and what's doing well and don't panic because you are not accustomed to good or great showing up for you, especially in relationships.

Everything isn't a fight or a chance to make your power statement. Some moments really are "YES, DEAR" moments and that goes for both sexes.

Respect

COOKING WITH LOVE
Start With A Good Base
Of Friendship:

1. Don't be so regulated and regimented about life that you forget to enjoy life. We went to Disney BEFORE our daughter was even born. It was a time for each of us to love our inner child and let 'em have fun!

2. Don't waste time and energy with silly resentments. The only people who get to be right all of the time are people who are alone with themselves and their own beliefs 24/7. No one is always right. No one wants to be with someone who is always right.

3. Some things are YOURS, not OURS! David has a comic book collection that's not going anywhere and Jamillah has a few stacks of mystery novels. We agree that we get to keep that part of ourselves.

4. Don't misdirect your anger about issues with other people onto your partner. That will live in your relationship and kill it from the inside.

5. Remember that you love your partner, even in a disagreement, because at some point the fight will be over, but you don't want the relationship to be.

6. Watch your mouth—it can say some beautiful things and undo some beautiful things—so guard it with your life and your love.

7. Understand your partner. When they are on you about spending, it's not about not wanting you to have the things you want. It's about them wanting to make sure that the family is taken care of, so you've got to be clear that your short-term excitement doesn't disregard their long-term vision.

END OF CHAPTER PLAYLIST

▶

Chapter Four — Unbreakable

1. **Unbreakable** by Alicia Keys

2. **Solid** by Ashford & Simpson

3. **Make It With You** by Ralfi Pagan

4. **Let's Stay Together** by Al Green

5. **A Heart Is A House for Love** by The Dells

CHAPTER FIVE

Can You Stand The Rain

Into everyone's life a little rain must fall, as the saying goes. We are certainly no different. Don't get us wrong, we were clearly being blessed, especially considering that we had only planned on running the play for one weekend, but then, its popularity surged beyond what we'd ever imagined. Wendy Williams had blessed it and hosted several times, even inviting her parents to see the show. And her on-air sidekick Charlamagne had joined the cast and had a chance to display his talents. Shaila and Lenny Green from 98.7 KISS-FM had blessed it. Nephew Tommy from the *Steve Harvey Morning Show* had come out and had audiences rolling in the aisles. Imhotep Gary Byrd, the legendary NYC radio personality, who'd been a supporter since *Platanos* was a novel, had also blessed us with his support. Our play was one of those events that had fans from eight to eighty. Business was good, and growing, but our family wasn't.

Be Fruitful and Multiply

When we decided, as husband and wife, that we were ready to have a family, we had no reason to believe it would be work. We knew it would take the physical, sexual work of creating a child, but that's one of the beauties of marriage. We really had no idea that there would be problems staying pregnant.

» *Jamillah*

We have suffered more than one miscarriage in our marriage and as the vessel that is used to hold and handle that baby into life, I felt like I was a failure. Something in me couldn't help but think that there must be something wrong with me.

David did everything he could in his loving, human and sometimes humorous way to assure me that I was beautiful and talented and that he believed in me and in our destiny as parents. He kept assuring me that we would be parents. He kept supporting me. But I had so many doubts about myself. How could I not? I wasn't having a problem getting pregnant; I was having problems staying pregnant.

» *David*

I remember the first time we found out something was wrong. We went to the doctor for a routine check-up early in the pregnancy. It was the first time they were going to do an ultrasound of the baby. We were excited and happy. We had no reason to think that anything was wrong. And then the doctor looked at the screen and looked at us. Powerless. That's how I felt. Powerless, because there was nothing I could do—our pregnancy was over. I would learn that I wasn't completely powerless though. I had the power to muster the strength to be supportive, and to be positive, and to help my wife stop blaming herself—because she definitely blamed herself. But I never wavered in being her biggest cheerleader. In the past, I'd said things that were stupid and ill-timed and hurt her feelings. But not then, not ever—because I believed in her, totally.

» *Jamillah*

After the grueling pain of my first miscarriage, I got pregnant again and I was really happy. We went for our initial six-week visit and all was well. There's a baby this time and there's a heartbeat and we are happy that we are finally going to be able to start our family. A few weeks later, we go back to the doctor for a follow-up visit and there's no heartbeat. It was a shock. We were starting to get angry because we just didn't understand. It was unbelievable and we were frustrated and scared and we didn't know what was happening.

I had to have the same procedure that I had to endure after the first miscarriage because my body wouldn't "naturally" miscarry. So we had to go through this painful emotional and physical process twice and still no babies. I started joining online communities to get information. We went to a fertility doctor and found out that there were no biological issues. So we just didn't know what to do. I cried a lot during this time, and I started to question myself and even thought that God might have not intended for me to be a mother. I even told David that he could leave me if he wanted because I didn't want to deny him the privilege being a father, and I wasn't sure what was going on with my body. We stayed together, of course, and just kept hoping and believing it would work out.

» David

After the second miscarriage, it took a long time for Jamillah to emotionally heal and feel like she was ready to try again. She was almost there; ready to try again, when we had one of those moments that can only be called a *sign*.

» Jamillah

At the time, we were running the play at a theater on 59th Street in Manhattan and David used our location as a convenient excuse to go to his favorite restaurant, *Benihana*. We had decided this night to take our stage manager there to celebrate his birthday, but it was just another reason for David to enjoy his favorite spot. Anyone who has ever been to *Benihana* knows that unlike other restaurants, it's conducive to sparking conversation with other people at your large communal table, even complete strangers.

I don't necessarily see signs as much as David does (I mean if he sees a squirrel collecting nuts in the Fall, he takes that as a sign winter is coming) but this day was amazing. I had recently told him that I was ready to try and get pregnant again, and he'd been asking me if I was sure, and we'd been going back and forth about it.

What sealed the deal for both of us that it was time to try again, was that while we were at *Benihana*, I was putting away some postcards that promoted *Platanos Y Collard Greens* and a man sitting next to us asked me what it was about because he'd heard of it. As we started talking, we found out that he was a specialist in Chinese medicine, specifically acupuncture and acupressure, and that his particular specialty was maintaining healthy pregnancies. He made the point to us that while Western medicine focused *on getting* pregnant, it doesn't spend the same energy *on staying* pregnant. Wow! That was a miracle. Really, who meets a doctor at a restaurant who specializes in Chinese medicine whose specialty is not getting pregnant but staying pregnant?

I definitely saw a sign in that.

» David

After her normally intense, exhaustive research and background check (she's like that, but it's a good thing) we decided to go ahead and get pregnant again, and the doctor we met at *Benihana* began treating her.

» Jamillah

He helped me take care of my body. I also took a lot better care of myself by taking time off from the production. David stepped up and handled 100 percent of the business, which is a daunting enough task for two people. For one person to become a two-man show was pretty exhausting, but he was so strong and so resourceful in the ways he just covered everything.

» David

Religious texts around the world compare women figuratively, and in some cases literally, to the earth. Never was that point driven home more for me than when Jamillah went on her mission to have a healthy pregnancy. She was determined to stay pregnant and have a healthy birth. She had what I can only describe as a religious zeal when it came to following her doctor's instructions.

Trust me, you have never seen a human being consume (not drink, but consume) so much water in one day, every day. She had been told that she had to keep herself properly irrigated like fertile earth and I never saw her during the entire pregnancy without at least a quart of water in her hand. Whether it was driving the car, eating dinner or turning the remote—that woman had a quart of water in her hand. I started to think that H_2O meant How 2 Overdose (on water). Even when she went to sleep she had a straw in her mouth connected to a quart of water.

» *Jamillah*

I know it was a little crazy, but those were Doctor's orders.

» *David*

I have to admit we were both a little paranoid about it. Going to the doctor for check-ups was a trip because we were always scared. We had the best OB/GYN but man did she point out every possible thing of concern and instruct us to have every test known to man.

» *Jamillah*

I know, she was thorough. And on top of that, David was a little neurotic. If we were at home and he felt my stomach and that baby wasn't getting down like James Brown—panic would set in. He would have me downing orange juice like it was going out of style. A few minutes later the sugar would hit the baby, and she would be doing back flips and break-dancing inside my tummy.

» *David*

Once in about her seventh or eighth month of pregnancy, I was at the theater because we had a show that night and Jamillah called from home panicked because she couldn't feel the baby moving. A short time later, we were at Methodist Hospital in Brooklyn, and she was hooked up to an EKG machine. Everything was fine. I even teased her about it, but I'd rather that she err on the side of caution than just dismiss it. She'd already said if it didn't work out this time, that was it, she couldn't emotionally handle losing another pregnancy. It's one of those moments as a man when you just have to relinquish, and just be supportive.

» *Jamillah*

The week I was due to give birth, we went to visit my doctor on a Monday. They measured how far I had dilated and were shocked that I wasn't in labor because I was so far along. They told us not to go home but instead to go for a walk and come back in a while. We weren't that far from Museum Mile, so we went to the Museum of Natural History. I think David was hoping the big animals would scare the girl out of me. A couple of hours later, we went back to the doctor and there was no change in my progress. I wasn't ready. So they sent me home.

Next day, nothing.

The day after that, nothing.

On Thursday, David had rehearsal in Manhattan and asked if he could go. I said nothing was happening, so he might as well.

» *David*

Ladies, remember she said nothing was happening so I might as well go. (MEN if this ever happens to you, stay your a** home!) I called her repeatedly from rehearsal. No news. I'm on the train coming out of the tunnel, riding over the Brooklyn Bridge when I call home, but the line is busy. I get off the

> **Pregnancy can teach you to let go** as a man, because you must. It can also teach you to be supportive, and put someone else first, to stop being so self-centered. **David**

train in Brooklyn and call home and she says, "Where the *hell* have you been?" And she *never* curses. "I've been calling you. The baby is coming! The contractions are six minutes apart!" I run home and we jump in a cab and it's like a scene out of a sitcom. As we're barreling up the West Side Highway, the contractions are coming closer together. Now they're five minutes, then four, then three. I called the doctor and she told the hospital to let us go straight into the delivery room. How Jamillah ever convinced me to be in the room I will never know, but I was there in my scrubs. I'll never forget my first words when my daughter was born, "Grandma!" I couldn't believe that she looked like my grandmother.

» Jamillah

Kaira came to life as the most beautiful, robust and joyful addition to our life. The process also healed my fears about myself as a woman. I didn't realize some of the issues I still had in me about me, but the journey of pregnancy brought up so much that needed healing and my husband was right there for the entire journey. He went with me to every doctor's visit. He not only joined me for a twelve-week natural child birth class called the Bradley Method, he did every assigned homework with joy. David's being there with me all the way is one of the many reasons why I love him. I know that he is always there—my support, my comfort and my rock.

Jamillah and David Five Months Pregnant

Daddy and Baby Kaira

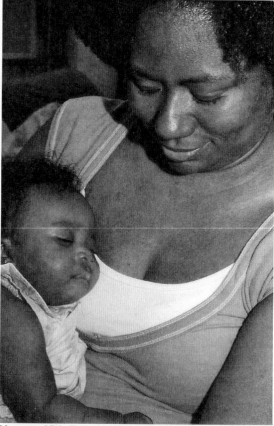

Mommy and Baby Kaira. photo: Curtis Corum

OUR KEY INGREDIENT

It's How You Help Each Other Through the Pain, Not the Pain, That Matters.

1 Cup of Support

1/2 Cup of Trust

1/2 Cup of Reliability

END·OF CHAPTER PLAYLIST

Chapter Five — Can You Stand The Rain

1. **Can You Stand The Rain** by New Edition

2. **0-o-h Child (Things Are Gonna Get Easier)** by The Five Stairsteps

3. **Lean on Me** by Bill Withers

4. **No One** by Alicia Keys

5. **To Be With You** by Joe Cuba

CHAPTER SIX

The Way You
Make Me Feel

❧

The conversation about what we love about each other and what's so special about being together is showing up at this point in the book, after talking about fights and disagreements and after the chapter about the painful things in life, because it's important to remember that you are in this together and that there are amazing things that you do for each other.

To be sure, we can all celebrate major moments, like the birth of a child or an anniversary, with big gestures. But, to us, the sweet and simple moments, are just as important—like brewing your honey a cup of hot peppermint tea, or giving your partner a soothing foot rub, or sliding in beside your love to watch a movie they love.

Sometimes, in all of the business and busyness of life, we forget to remember the little things, the moments that matter and that keep you in love when you are working to pay bills or dashing out the door to get to an event because the babysitter showed up late. You have to take the time to do the things that you did when you dated because that's the person who was involved in the courting, wooing and winning of the heart of the person you are in a relationship with now. So keep courting, wooing and winning their heart.

>> *David*

This is the God's honest truth—I am more attracted to my wife today than I was when we met. And when we met I was very attracted to her. I love everything about her. Her hair. Her super-model boots. The royal West African garb she wore in Senegal. The fact that I think she can't dance, but that she loves to. The way she's turning our daughter into a miniature of herself, but still letting her develop her own little personality. The way she picks me up when I'm down. It's a corny line from a movie but she "completes me". I remember when we first celebrated my birthday and she gave me **two** birthday cards, one that was serious, about how much she loves me, and one that was silly, addressed to Davey Lambchops. That's who she is: The serious businesswoman and the sweet girl.

When we first met, she lived in California and I lived in New York and I wanted her to know she had my heart (and I wanted to capture hers) so I put together a collection of songs about us. I told her to expect a package. Even though I paid for overnight delivery, it didn't get there. The next day it still hadn't arrived and I thought it was lost in the mail. Her interest was building because she didn't know what I had sent and she was curious. The next day I had a message on my home phone, "Dude, I'm floating!" she sang in her happiest voice. We kept that tape (yes, there were still cassette tapes not that long ago) in the tape deck of our old car for years. *Hope That We Can Be Together Soon* by Sharon Paige and Harold Melvin & The Blue Notes (featuring Teddy Pendergrass) was our theme song during the long distance portion of our relationship.

» *Jamillah*

I still get goose bumps and I still float whenever I hear that song.

» *David*

Make sure that the love of your life knows that they are still the love in your life.

It is so important to remain the person you were when you were dating, even years into your relationship. Maybe you can't always find the time to make romantic dinners, but you can put some romance into the carry-out that you picked up on the way home. Candles always work. Music always helps. You can do the things that you used to do and even create a few new rituals, especially when you remember that you want to make sure that the love of your life knows that they are still the love in your life.

I can't ice skate—at all! But I had the impression that Jamillah wanted to go ice skating in Bryant Park, so I surprised her one day. We were holding on for dear life along the rails of the ice skating rink. But fellas, we're competitive, so as these kids are flying by doing triple axles, I started thinking *it can't be that hard.* So I pushed off and ventured out; I could only push off with one foot, but it was fun. Fun, new and exciting with my wife, especially when I tried to snatch her in my arms, spin her and tell her I love her—which was the way it appeared in my head. But on the ice that day, it didn't quite go down like that.

» Jamillah

It's true. From the beginning, he has been surprising me. When we decided to get married, it was a big deal for me. I knew that I wanted to look pretty that day. But David made me feel beautiful.

It was May 5, (Cinco de Mayo), our wedding day. I still remember how much I cried that day. I was already happy and already blessed to be marrying this amazing man. He was talented and smart and attractive. But when he surprised me (shocked me) and sang to me at our wedding, I think I cried all of my make-up off. David doesn't sing. He doesn't fancy himself a singer and he wasn't hiding some great voice. He wanted to give me a song and he presented it at the ceremony, and blew me away. It was the most amazing thing anyone had ever done for me.

» David

I can't sing. It's not me being modest. It's just not my gift. But for our wedding, I wanted to do something special for her. I found this amazing song called *Queen Bee* by Taj Mahal, a great blues musician whose music I love. The song spoke to me and I wanted to give it to my *Queen Bee* as a gift. I worked with the band and we did it live for her, and as much as guys don't ever want to be in a position of making a fool of them-selves, (especially me), I was glad to be a fool for love, in love. It made her cry and she knows that I meant it from my soul. I didn't want it to be "our song" or a moment that was about anything other than her knowing that I love her so much that

I would do anything, including sing a song in public that says how much I love her.

» *Jamillah*

Even though David is truly my knight in shining armor, he isn't exactly brimming with gentlemanly manners. David does not pull out chairs or open car doors for me. When we first started dating and we would go to restaurants, he would order first. I used to think, "Wow, this man is not chivalrous at all." What was odd was that I'd spent so much of my early adulthood trying to make sure that I didn't let a man into my life who was trying to control me, so I actually didn't like any of those gestures. But now I think I want some of them, or maybe I'm just making room for them now that I'm with the right man.

Relax Yourself

» *David*

Sometimes there is a kernel of truth in first impressions, and my first impression of Jamillah when I met her was that she was too tightly wound and there's still truth in that.

» *Jamillah*

Oh really!

» *David*

Yes! Before I met Jamillah I'd never even heard of or imagined anyone getting so stressed over vacations, both taking them and planning them. She would become so stressed over vacations that "relax yourself" became my mantra for her.

» *Jamillah*

You had taken maybe one vacation in your life before meeting me.

» *David*

That's true. But my point remains. This is a woman who would work like a maniac right up until the split second before we got on the plane, then collapse on the hotel bed and actually believe she was recuperating. She would research and investigate every possible scenario of every possible vacation on the computer at home, like she was working on a five-year business plan, and become exhausted and frazzled.

» *Jamillah*

Trip Advisor is awesome!

» *David*

After several stressful vacation planning adventures, I told her, "I can't take it anymore. I'll plan this vacation." Fifteen minutes later, I had booked flights and a hotel in the Caribbean.

Vacations

I'm a Pisces, a fish; so a vacation to me means water. He's a Capricorn, a goat; a trip to him to the mountains is fine. He even thinks a lake can substitute for the ocean. A lake? Really? **Jamillah**

» *Jamillah*

That's what I love about my husband. I love the way he makes me feel. He considers me, the person that I am. He doesn't just rely on the "do this and girls will like it" ways that guys can romance women. His being there, as a shoulder to lean on or being the one who makes me laugh is what makes me smile. He doesn't tease me about reality shows. (And will even watch them occasionally.)

Or he has fun with me while I eat my buffalo wings, even though he hates them.

He would laugh at how stressed out I'd get while planning vacations. And, he's right; I would get totally stressed out because I was trying to make sure everyone was happy. Since he couldn't take seeing me so stressed out, he planned the next vacation, handled all of the details (which drove me crazy because I am so accustomed to it). But everything was fine. I just had to lay back and enjoy it. This was one of those times when I had to get out of my head—and he has been so beautiful about helping me live in the world and not be overwhelmed by my thoughts of what needs to be done next. Oh and Aruba was amazing!

I am getting to pay attention to myself and see what I need to feel loved and supported as a woman.

I love that David is a strong force in my life without having to be a strong presence, meaning he doesn't have to prove that he is my man or the man in the relationship. The way that he loves me makes me know that he gets me and pays attention to me.

Now, I am getting to pay attention to myself and see what I need to feel loved and supported as a woman. Maybe I do want those roses and romance in the traditional way sometimes, especially now that I can believe (because I am living it) that I would marry a man who loves me in such a special way.

I'm blessed to have a man who knows exactly when to tell me to slow down and supports me when I do it. He helps me to unravel my need to structure everything, including vacations, and he's shown me that I can slow down and still get all of the important things done. He's also helped me see that not everything is *that* important.

SHE SAYS:
"LET YOUR FLOWER BLOOM"

When I was younger, I was spending so much time proving who I wasn't and what I wouldn't accept and being clear about what a guy couldn't do for me, that I think I forgot about me. I forgot to think about what I did want and what I could offer.

Now that I am in a marriage that has grown from a relationship that's about love and balance and mutual respect, I am discovering that I might actually like flowers and chocolates as signs of romance.

» *David*

Well that's good to know.

» *Jamillah*

I am also discovering that if I have changed my mind, I need to tell my husband.

I have to open myself up to that new truth and let him know surprising me with chocolates and flowers would put a smile on my face and some sunshine in my heart. Romantic comedies make us think we aren't really in love if we if we don't finish each other's sentences, which really means reading each other's minds. I'm learning to not simply rely on him to read my mind but to talk about myself and my needs and what I want from and in my life and what I'd like to experience.

It's okay to change your mind, but when you do... remember to let your partner know.

Make Yours a Happy Home

» David

Sometimes you don't even realize that you are speaking things into existence. You may know that when you are saying something, you hope that someone is listening, but many times we talk about our hopes, dreams, aspirations and interests and feel that we are just hoping aloud. We don't realize that someone is listening. It feels really amazing when someone surprises you by doing something that makes you realize that not only is someone actually listening but without you even knowing they are actively working to help bring your dreams to fruition.

When we first met, my wife and I hung on each other's every word. We are still listening to each other and that's what makes us work in so many ways. Yes, it's great for business and partnership, but it's really something when it literally hits close to home and catches you by surprise.

Last year for Valentine's Day, we were walking around the neighborhood and I noticed that we were taking a long, exaggerated route because she didn't want me to know where we were going. To my surprise, we ended up at a studio in Brooklyn where they teach an "Absolute Beginners" class for *Capoeira*, which combines elements of martial arts, sports, and music from the Afro-Brazilian culture. I have been talking about wanting to take classes for a while. I had been working out to prepare myself, but I hadn't signed up for the classes, partly because I thought I had to be in optimal shape because it's rigorous and partly because I stay so busy.

What I didn't realize was that she'd heard me and had taken concrete steps to getting me started by signing me up for the Absolute Beginners class. As much as I love to run my mouth, it's a beautiful thing when I realize that she's listening. Unlike me, (where I can get stuck on an idea in my head for years), she'll take the initiative to make it happen. I realize it was this same energy that turned *Platanos* into a play; she'd helped me take it from a possibility as a play to a living, breathing award winning reality.

That's what she does for me consistently, turns my dreams into reality. For years, I'd been tooting my own horn about wanting to take trumpet lessons. I love the instrument so much that I have even written a play that includes a role for a young trumpet player. (Part of my fascination is that holding a trumpet looks so cool! It's shallow but it's true.) Sometimes that instrument just speaks to me.

Romance is about keeping the fire burning, not just getting it started.

Once again, she got me lessons and I am still taking those lessons today. I never knew that you had to use so many facial muscles in order to play the trumpet. They are the same muscles in your face that you use to smile. So every time I smile, it hurts and the cool thing is that when it hurts, I remember that I am taking trumpet lessons. It's no longer a bucket list item or on my things-to-do list. It's a part of my actual life. It's a fulfilling experience that I get to do for me. (And if you will allow a father to brag for a moment, we were both shocked to discover that our three-year-old daughter could blow the trumpet! I was so amazed. And my teacher was speechless. So now my daughter and I have something more to share.)

*Love isn't a destination. It's a journey of
Tuesday afternoons and Sunday mornings. If you
pay attention along the way, it will tell you just what to
do in order to show someone that you still care.*

Romance
*One of Jamillah's sweet
romantic gestures:*
Jamillah stayed up until 2 a.m.
to bake David a butternut squash
pie for his birthday, although
she had never baked a pie in her
life, which is why she was in a
hot kitchen way past midnight.

*One of David's sweet
romantic gestures:*
After hearing an ad on the radio,
David surprised Jamillah with
all-day spa treatments at Spa
Castle, a Korean style fabulous
multi-level, multi-sauna spa.

Being with the right person for you will make you want to find real ways to romance them and not just fall back on the okey-doke. Paying attention pays off. You'll want to notice the things that make her eyes light up, even while you're walking down the street on the way home. Register those things in your brain. And when you need to—or just want to shower love on your love (or get out of the doghouse), take cues from all that you've been listening to and observing, and cater to your love. That's romance.

HE SAYS:
"ACCENTUATE THE POSITIVE"

I always knew that humor was important in any relationship, but I now appreciate even more how important it is to keep her laughing. Laughter can brighten up any day and lighten up those moments when you forget something or when you don't always present the best you. Keeping her laughing has been essential to reminding both of us that we are friends, and that we get to be friendly with each other just because.

There's nothing sweeter than doing something just because I was thinking about her and that voice in my head said "remember, she said she wants flowers" or "Hey, I bet Jamillah would love this book or this candy bar." That voice is your own voice telling you that this is what you wanted in a relationship and these are the simple, sincere things that you need to do in order to keep it, hold it and continue it.

David singing *Queen Bee* to Jamillah at the Wedding

OUR KEY INGREDIENT

℮⅍

Paying Attention
Pays Off

2 cups of Paying Attention

1 cup of Lightheartedness

1 cup of Giving

1 cup of Thoughtfulness

Most of us want to be heard, understood, and appreciated, and have someone with whom to share the places, people, things, and activities that we cherish.

If your partner loves basketball, then basketball is your way of getting to know them. If your honey likes romantic movies, then stop being macho, get a box of tissues, and commence to crying with her. Whatever works, you have to be willing to work it and that means paying attention.

There's nothing worse than thinking you are being romantic by bringing your lady flowers and she's allergic. (This is not a hypothetical; this has happened.) You would have known that if you were paying attention instead of relying on media gimmicks for clues on "what a woman wants" and they don't know *your* woman.

Romance is a personal and intimate act that always considers the person you are trying to romance and not just the topic of romance. When it comes to the one who is the object of your affections, you must become keenly attuned to what floats their boat.

Romance

COOKING WITH LOVE

Flavor Your Relationship
with Romance:

1. Make dinner. If you can't cook, make reservations.

2. When he really wants to watch the game, dish up some of his favorite munchies, then cozy up along side him until the final buzzer sounds.

3. Listen to what she talks to her friends about and take notes. If you get stumped, ask her friends. There are nuggets in them there hills (and tips).

4. Pay attention to something your partner wants to get done and hasn't yet and see how you can help that come true.

5. Offer to drive or do dishes, something that they usually do but sometimes complain about.

6. Keep it simple (and silly). Keep comedy in your life. As they say: Happy wife, happy life. Happy husband, good loving.

7. When you want something, just say it. Don't hem and haw and play around with words waiting for them to get it. It's not that deep. If you are in the mood for a certain food or a specific movie, JUST SAY IT!

8. Stay young at heart and you will be young at home. Go to an amusement park, exercise, play basketball together, go to the circus, learn a "young" dance move—have you seen First Lady Michelle Obama doing the *Dougie*?

9. Laugh at yourself and each other! Sometimes, in love, we say some stupid stuff.

END OF CHAPTER PLAYLIST

▶

Chapter Six — The Way You Make Me Feel

1. **The Way You Make Me Feel** by Michael Jackson

2. **You Send Me** by Sam Cooke

3. **Adore** by Prince

4. **The Light** by Common

5. **Fool For You** (featuring Melanie Fiona) by Cee Lo Green

CHAPTER SEVEN

Always Be My Baby

W e wanted to write a chapter about all the reasons we fit so well together. But when we thought about it, the central visual and actual manifestation of it is our beautiful daughter—she's the perfect combination of us both. She's her mother's insightful and her father's funny; her mother's love of baking and her father's love of storytelling. Our daughter is the best of us come to life, standing in front of us, every day. She reminds us that we have been brought together by something Greater for something great.

Children are a perfect addition to a relationship. When you look at your children, they will remind you, in their actions and their smiles of all of the best parts of your being together.

We dedicate this chapter to our daughter and, to all sons and daughters who are the living and breathing reminders to parents that love is a beautiful thing.

» David

My little girl is the perfect combination of our love, in remarkable ways.

She has the forehead of my mother and the hair of her mother's mother. My eyes. The cutest dimples in the world—just like my wife's. I'll never forget the moment she was born. (Even if I still, I don't know how my wife convinced me to be in the delivery room!) I was shocked by how much she looked like my grandmother.

When we brought her home, I noticed that she had the perfect little delicate chin just like Jamillah's grandmother. And much to my surprise, I found out (thanks to my nine-year-old cousin) that she had "elf ears" just like her daddy. When I asked about "elf ears," this precious nine-year-old said, "Yeah, you didn't know you had elf ears?" All I could say was, "No, and I could have gone my whole life not knowing if you hadn't said anything!"

It's been incredible that one little girl could be such a combination of two hearts joined as one. But when I think about it, that's exactly what she is. Like our love, every day for her is full of new adventure. Like our love, her joy is limitless. I will never forget the first time I came home and she came running to the door to greet me, hugging me yelling "Daddy!" I didn't know that a human being could be so happy! And then I looked at the wall and saw a photo of my wife crying tears of joy on our wedding day, and remembered how happy we were then and how happy I am to have Jamillah in my life. She's my partner, my best friend and confidante. She (really) completes me.

My uncle, who was the best man at our wedding, commented as she walked down the aisle, "I am so proud of you, she is so right for you. You two are the perfect combination."

» *Jamillah*

Our daughter Kaira is such a blessing. She reminds me every day to slow down (have you ever tried rushing out of the house with a three-year-old? Just add twenty more minutes to your schedule because she has to grab one more toy, go to the bathroom (after you put her coat on), and put on her shoes herself. She reminds me every day to laugh, to sing and to dance.

She is so beautiful, so smart and she has the most kind and caring spirit. She truly is a gift. I feel like we communicated even before she was born. And we had a bond from when she was in the womb.

David and I have grown closer (if that's possible) through the birth of our daughter, not just because of the hardships of our lost pregnancies, but in taking care of her together, in raising our family and making decisions together, we discover new things about each other and we discover new parts of ourselves in her. And that's a beautiful thing.

Kaira definitely inspires me to work to be the best that I can be so that, in turn, David and I can continue to be not perfect, but perfect for each other and for her.

Kaira in her Pink Party Dress

Lamb Family Vacation 2011

Lamb Family

Kaira

OUR KEY INGREDIENT

Be Grateful

2 Cups of Thankfulness

1 Cup of Humility

It is a blessing to remember that your child is a glorious gift. If we had to actually track what it takes out of millions of possibilities, to blend the best of each of us to create life, we would never forget life is a miracle.

When you realize that life is so precious, it will give you strength when daily living gets too heavy and your debts are way too high. It will make you reconsider every argument, every fight and every time you feel like you need to win, remember that if you have children, you've already won. Stand up for that love and look at it when you see those children and remember that you are all that they have and you are teaching them joy and happiness, self-worth and self expression. Children are the deepest parts of ourselves, released to us outside of us to remind us of who we are and all that we can be. Remember that they will leave you one day and if you teach them well, they will become you—bigger, stronger and more empowered. And if we handle that divine charge in the right way, being parents can serve to make us better people overall.

Remember to love your children and while doing so, remember to thank each other for the gift you share. It will make the rest of it all seem so mediocre next to the miracle of life itself.

Gratitude

COOKING WITH LOVE

Teach, Support and Unconditionally Love Your Children:

1. Love your children, unconditionally.

2. Remember that they are looking to you and at you for everything. Teach them well.

3. Don't forget that they are always looking to see if you are looking at them. Smile and laugh with them and let them know they matter.

4. As a couple, together, take the time to do things with your children. But also make just mommy-and-me time, and just daddy-and-me time.

5. Be grateful.

END OF CHAPTER PLAYLIST

▶

Chapter Seven — Always Be My Baby

1. **Always Be My Baby** by Mariah Carey

2. **Dat Dere** by Oscar Brown Jr.

3. **What A Wonderful World**
   by Louis Armstrong

4. **Princesa** by Frank Reyes

5. **Just The Two Of Us** by Will Smith

Bonus Track
6. **Isn't She Lovely** by Stevie Wonder

CHAPTER EIGHT

Love and Happiness

When we were teenagers we all (or many of us) loved to ride rollercoasters; the twists and turns, the highs and lows, the thrills and chills were irresistible. What made these manic rides bearable was that when we got on board we knew where the ride was going, and how long it would take.

The rollercoaster of love likewise has twists and turns, highs and lows, and thrills and chills. But unlike an amusement park thrill, on the ride of love we don't necessarily know where it's going or how long it's going to last. For many people, that sense of not knowing is frightening. But consider for a moment that rather than being frightening, love's mysterious journey can be a thrilling adventure that puts a smile on your face and brings joy to your soul.

When we began this adventure in love together we had no idea where it would lead us (we weren't even sure what state we would be living in), we had no idea we would visit the pyramids in Mexico or see Africa for the first time when we visited Senegal, or be invited to perform at the NAACP's 100th Anniversary. And we certainly had no idea that Judge Alex would be officiating a wedding at our play, but that's exactly what's happened. We've not only been blessed to share our passion with others, but to have others share their passion with us.

We smile every time we remember the first time a nervous young man wanted to propose to his girlfriend at the play. David snuck into the audience toward the end of the show and tapped the young man on the shoulder and then ushered him back to the dressing room to change into the suit he'd smuggled in without his future bride knowing. We're sure that while he was backstage changing, she was wondering what was taking him so long in the bathroom. When the curtain call was over, and the spotlight came up on him, we'll never forget her excitement or his. Talk about a standing ovation! We've been blessed to have witnessed several proposals at the show. After all, it is a romantic comedy.

We've even been blessed to have had a couple who felt that the play was so special to them, they asked to be married at the show. So we had a wedding, complete with bridesmaids and groomsmen, and TV's Judge Alex witnessing their vows. A Universal Motown recording artist, London, also crooned while the couple walked down the aisle. We want to thank all those who've shared their love with us by sharing our love with you.

Where sometimes you feel vulnerable and want to run and live out your new self in front of someone new, the truth of being able to go to the next level is being man enough and woman enough to stick and stay.

There are so many powerful lessons, important lessons that we have learned about our love and ourselves as we have gone through the process of writing this book.

This chapter is really about being able to draw together all of the lessons that we have learned that don't need a lot of explanation. They just are and their importance is pretty clear. These lessons are ones that we both understand and respect.

We are one, as a couple, as a family, as a woman and as a man, and what we've learned along the way is that you've got to be willing to learn the lessons—even when you don't like the lessons. Being willing to learn the lessons has helped us help each other become more of the person we were always intended to be.

It's weird, but true, being in a relationship is about being able to let yourself grow.

So breathe and throw your hands up, like you would on a rollercoaster. You got on this ride on purpose, so just enjoy it—and where you need to, just scream. Let out the fears and the frustrations, but stay on the ride!

OUR (NOT SO) SECRET
BONUS KEY INGREDIENT

❧

Love

A Whole Bunch of Love — Love and Happiness are not elusive. They are accessible. But they begin with a ready, willing and able self strong enough to make the journey and take the trip.

Along the road, you gain self-awareness, self-knowledge and perhaps a greater sensibility.

We wanted to do something special for this book; to speak from a place in our hearts that we had never spoken from before. We wanted to speak to love and not just to each other.

We decided to write a love letter to "Love" itself with the hope that you and your partner will realize how important it is to keep love in mind and on your minds—so that when you struggle, you remember that you are struggling for love and it's definitely worth the work.

Here's to love:

Dear Love,

I love you. I truly do. I love how you make me feel giddy. I love how you make me smile. I love how you make me feel happy even on a cold rainy day. I love how you make me look forward to even the smallest things… watching a tv show or sharing a joke. I love you.

I am so sorry for wasting time…being inside my head and not just letting go. I promise to always open my heart so I can always be near you and near the joy that you bring.

I love you,

Jamillah & David

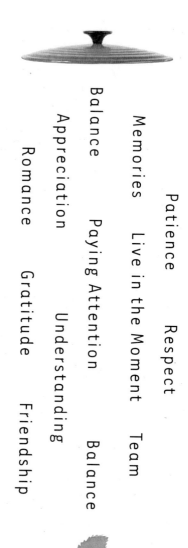

Patience   Respect

Memories   Live in the Moment   Team

Balance

Appreciation   Paying Attention

Romance   Gratitude   Understanding

Balance

Friendship

COOKING WITH LOVE

Lessons That We Have Lived, Learned And Are Still Learning Along The Way:

1. Pay attention to signs, they are trying to tell you something.

2. Don't always focus on your own needs. Realize that in helping your partner, you help yourself.

3. Don't be so judgmental about yourself. You did it. It's over. Move forward.

4. Change is a daily operation. If you don't do the work to stop yourself from sliding back to behaviors that doomed past relationships, you will fall back and doom your present relationship.

5. Be willing to compromise. Go to places that mean something to you as a couple and individually. If your partner really wants to go somewhere that's not on your "must see" list, go anyway. Support their interest and try to enjoy the trip through their eyes.

6. Be clear about what you each do well. (Yes your mother could cook, but she's not your mother.)

7. Establish boundaries. If you need to get the day off your chest, something that happened on the subway or at the store tell your partner—and ask for a specific amount of time (10 minutes or so). When it's done, let it be done. Your partner isn't a dumping ground for your drama.

8. Listen. Encourage. Don't berate. Help your partner accomplish the goals that they have in mind but don't dismiss them if they fall short of those goals. If you toss a stink bomb at them, be ready for the smell to take over the entire house.

9. Support each other in what you do well. If you don't do laundry, at least take the clothes to the dry cleaner.

10. Don't let whatever you dealt with during the day disturb your time together. If you need a comedy or a shower to get the day off of you, do it so you can start fresh at home.

11. Live in the moment. As Dale Carnegie writes in
    How to Stop Worrying and Start Living "Shut tight
    the iron doors to regrets about yesterday and fears
    about tomorrow!"

12. Don't carry grudges. They're too heavy.

13. Speak the vision that you have for your family.
    Talk about things that are important to your vision
    of your family so that you are sure that you're both
    on the same page.

14. You can read each other's hearts, but not each
    other's minds.

15. Say only what you mean—and keep the rest
    to yourself.

16. Don't take yourself or any situation too seriously
    or so seriously that it wastes time!

17. Discover new things with each other. Be willing to
    be adventurous in every way.

18. Don't misrepresent your anger. If you are upset about something, speak on that without bringing a thousand and one other unrelated things into it.

19. Get rid of the negative voices in your head about yourself. It takes a lot of work, but it's worth it. Pick up Don Miguel Ruiz's *The Voice of Knowledge: A practical guide to inner peace.*

20. Treat each day like it's new, and be grateful to and for each other.

END OF CHAPTER PLAYLIST

▶

Chapter Eight – Love and Happiness

1. **Love and Happiness** by Al Green

2. **As** by Stevie Wonder

3. **The Best of My Love** by The Emotions

4. **Spend My Life With You** by Eric Benet

5. **Always and Forever** by Heatwave

TURN THE PAGE FOR A PEEK AT
OUR NEXT PROJECT, PUBLISHED BY
JAMILLAH AND DAVID LAMB

KING OF THE WORLD

By David Lamb

DAVID LAMB

KING OF THE WORLD

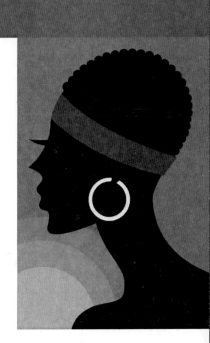

It was a long complicated road for Rose and Set college sweethearts, best friends, partners, superstar power couple. When they fell in love, Set was the biggest nerd on campus with glasses so big he looked like an owl hunting for prey—until Rose gave him the ultimate makeover.

Now he's the biggest superstar on the planet; a trend setting fashion mogul music producer. And together they are advisers to the Obama campaign. They have it all! Until he betrays her and throws it all away. Now, tonight on the biggest night of their lives as they share the spotlight before an audience of millions, after not having spoken in three years, will he give it all up for a second chance at love.

Prologue

I t had been a long, twisting, complicated road for Rose
and Set—college sweethearts, best friends, partners, power
couple, *exes*.

Whenever Rose reminisced about their time together
her feelings ran from exhilaration to disappointment; which
is precisely why she tried not to think of them too often. The
world didn't know it—and probably wouldn't believe it—but
she was the one who had given *him* his cool, or had at least
given Set the confidence to discover his cool. She couldn't help
the tiny smile that widened as she remembered the first time she
saw him awkwardly walking around campus: lost; desperately
in need of a haircut and for some reason wearing glasses so
thick and big that he looked like an owl hunting for prey. And
that was just from the neck up. Below that—the mismatched
dress socks...with sandals...weren't helping his case either! He
was just plain pitiful.

And now, now, *he* was the biggest music superstar on
the planet, the epitome of cool.

"Incredible," she whispered as she smiled to herself and
shook her head dissolving away the happy memories of those
innocent college days and bringing her back to the present.

Gazing at the striking skyline of the City of Angels from the back of a sleek, luxurious limousine, Rose nervously checked her hair in the mirror for the dozenth time in the last half-dozen minutes. *Everything's gonna be fine girl* she encouraged herself, as she squirmed uncomfortably, feeling awkward, not from the plush interior, but from this day's incredible irony. It was exactly three years to the day she'd angrily walked out of his life, and tonight she and Set were both nominated for *Awards*. *God's certainly got a sense of humor*, she laughed.

As for herself, she'd never planned on being nominated for anything. Change had come to her life so fast that the past three years seemed like a blur. And now there was a chance that in a few hours she would be standing at the podium with millions of eyes on her. Butterfly swarms fluttered in her stomach as she arrived at *The Awards*. Despite her nervous excitement, Rose looked magnificent in her Michelle Obama inspired custom-fitted *Isabel Toledo* black sheath dress. From the moment Rose saw the first Black First Lady wearing it she knew it was for her.

Rose had to admit she'd always loved Mrs. Obama's style. From the instant they met on the campaign trail Rose thought that Michelle had always stolen the spotlight. She was so proud of Michelle being a fellow Chicago girl. She and Set did everything they could to put her and Barack in the White House. And their enthusiasm was rewarded when just a few short months after diving into the campaign, Rose and Set stood on the floor of the Democratic Convention applauding and cheering like the revolution had been televised as Obama officially accepted the nomination. They were both so proud, feeling, rightly, that they had helped make history happen. For months they'd traveled non-stop across the country, hosting rallies and putting on concerts, doing all they could to help to get out the vote.

Then, on the anniversary of the day they'd first kissed, Barack Obama was elected president of the United States, and Rose and Set were ecstatic to be in the political mix. That night as Rose gazed dreamily into Set's eyes, sparkling as they did when he was happy and filled with hope, she felt complete. As he held her in his arms under the clear skies with the fresh summer air blowing in off of Lake Michigan everything seemed possible. They were so full of hope; so blissfully in love that Set longed to tug the moon from its lofty place in the heavens and place it on her chestnut-colored ring finger like an astonishing colossal pearl where its luminous glow would perpetually cast light on Rose's beauty. As they danced under the stars in the warmth of love and happiness their hearts embraced like long-lost lovers and Rose felt her spirit joyously soar.

That night in Chicago neither Rose nor Set had any idea how much and how quickly things would change. Nor had they any hint that by the arrival of *this* night—the biggest night of each of their lives—they would have spent thirty-six whole months not having spoken a single word to each other.

As she stepped out of the back of the limousine and walked the red carpet while the paparazzi started popping away, Rose thought about everything that had led up to this moment, though she was anxious on the inside, on the outside she smiled as if she wasn't the least bit nervous while praying for two things—*don't let me freeze in front of all these people, and please, please don't let me run into Set.*

ACKNOWLEDGMENTS

We would like to thank our parents and our families, the Muhammads, Lambs, Conways, Wards and Corums for teaching us about life and for their love and support.

We thank Kevin Taylor for helping us bring our vision to life. We thank Cynthia Rae for her amazing support.

I would like to acknowledge my husband, my partner in life, and my forever love, David. You have bought me so much joy and I look forward to laughing, crying, hugging and dancing with love forever with you. And to my mother, Anisah Muhammad, I want to acknowledge my appreciation of your patience and your love, now that I have a daughter who is me reincarnated I am more grateful than ever.

I would like to acknowledge my wife, my sunshine who warms my everyday and puts a song in my heart. I am yours forever.

We thank our daughter Kaira for being who she is... the most beautiful little girl who brings light, love and laughter wherever she goes.

We would also like to thank all of the wonderful actors, directors and stage managers who have worked with us over the years, your talent, inspiration and hard work have been truly appreciated. We would also like to acknowledge David's cousin, Wayne.

DAVID AND JAMILLAH LAMB

are the husband and wife team who own Between The Lines
Productions, Inc., a company they developed in 2003 to inspire
and bring the joy of laughter to people. David was born in Queens,
NY and raised in public housing in Astoria, Queens. He attended
the Woodrow Wilson School of Public and International Affairs at
Princeton University and New York University School of Law. He
is the playwright of *Platanos Y Collard Greens*, a piece that grew out of his
experiences in Queens. Jamillah Lamb grew up in Chicago, in the
same neighborhood as First Lady Michelle Obama. After earning
her Bachelor's degree in economics from Wesleyan University, she
went on to Harvard University, where she gained her Masters degree
in Public Policy. She uses this background in the daily operations
of Between The Lines Productions, Inc. Jamillah always loved
theater and shares David's passion for creative work. David loves
being married business partners and parenting with Jamillah.
They live in Brooklyn with their wonderful little girl.

www.acoupleoflambs.com